Aleene's
CRAFT QUICKIES

Oxmoor
House.

Library of Congress Catalog Number: 95-68298
Hardcover ISBN: 0-8487-1449-0
Softcover ISBN: 0-8487-1463-6
Manufactured in the United States of America
Third Printing 1996

Aleene's™ is a registered trademark of Artis, Inc.
Trademark Registration #1504878
Aleene's™ is used by permission of Artis, Inc.

Designs by Heidi Borchers

Editor-in-Chief: Nancy J. Fitzpatrick
Senior Crafts Editor: Susan Ramey Cleveland
Senior Editor, Editorial Services: Olivia Kindig Wells
Art Director: James Boone

Aleene's Craft Quickies

Editor: Margaret Allen Price
Assistant Art Director: Cynthia R. Cooper
Editorial Assistant: Janica Lynn York
Copy Editor: L. Amanda Owens
Senior Photographer: John O'Hagan
Photographer: Keith Harrelson
Photo Stylist: Connie Formby
Illustrator: Kelly Davis
Senior Production Designer: Larry Hunter
Publishing Systems Administrator: Rick Tucker
Production and Distribution Director: Phillip Lee
Production Manager: Gail Morris
Associate Production Manager: Theresa L. Beste
Production Assistant: Marianne Jordan

Contents

Quick Decorative Accents   6
Add a handmade touch to your decor with projects like no-sew pillows and pretty picture frames.

Page 14

Fun with Fashion   38
Craft fashionable garments, accessories, and jewelry with the designs in this chapter.

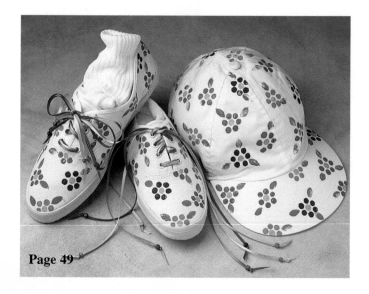

Page 49

Page 86

Page 139

Page 100

Aleene   *Heidi*   *Tiffany*

Introduction

If you love crafting as much as Heidi, Tiffany, and I do, you'll enjoy the wealth of beautiful designs featured here. My daughter Heidi has created a treasure trove of designs that offer you a world of ways to express your creativity.

You may have seen Heidi on "Aleene's Creative Living," a television show about crafting produced by my daughter Tiffany. Heidi specializes in what I call junk crafting. I think she is the foremost authority on turning things you would normally throw away into gorgeous crafts. Brown grocery bags and empty boxes are just a couple of "trash" items that you'll see used in these projects. So gather your supplies and get ready to turn your trash into treasure.

Heidi has organized these special designs into four chapters. The first chapter, "Quick Decorative Accents," features crafts you can make and use to decorate your home. You'll find lots of ways to add handmade touches to any room with these projects. Be sure to look at the Burnt Brown Bag Wind Chimes (pages 26 and 27). Wind chimes are a great housewarming gift, but they cost a fortune.

You can make this chiming owl for far less.

Turn to "Fun with Fashion" to update your wardrobe with a bit of craft magic. There are plenty of ideas, from casual T-shirts and sneakers to an elegant black dress and fancy shoe clips.

I have always believed it is very important to begin early to teach children to craft. Don't send them out of the room while you are working on your handmade treasures; teach them to craft with you. Many of the designs in "Crafts for Kids" are appropriate for children from toddlers to teens.

We crafters take special pride in displaying our handiwork during the holidays. Of course, Heidi gives Christmas top billing since it's our favorite holiday. But in "Holiday Magic" you'll also find projects for Halloween and Easter, as well as a cute birthday party idea with a clown theme.

Before you begin your crafts, please take a look at the section called "Crafting with Heidi." You'll learn all the basic crafting techniques you need to get started on these great crafts.

Wishing you hours of creativity,

Aleene

Page 40

Page 22

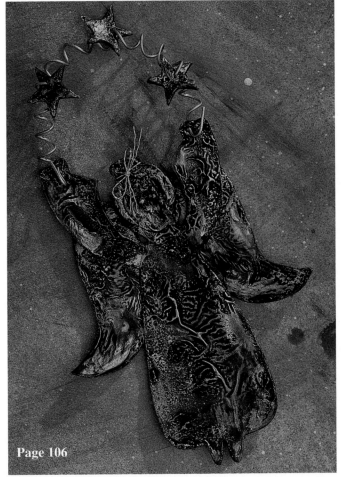

Page 106

Quick Decorative Accents

From no-sew throw pillows and burnt brown bag candle holders to seasonal flags and a variety of picture frames, in this chapter you'll find a wealth of ways to adorn your home with handmade crafts.

Reverse Collage Vases

Glue silk flowers or gift wrap cutouts inside a vase for an elegant tabletop statement.

Materials (for 1 vase)

Silk flowers and leaves (Use flat flowers for best results.) or sunburst motifs cut from gift wrap
Paper napkins: flower motif gossamer (very thin) or celestial motif
Sponge paintbrush
Aleene's Reverse Collage™ Glue
Glass or plastic vase
Aleene's Right-On Finish™ (optional)

Directions

1 Remove all plastic parts from silk flowers and leaves. Iron flowers and leaves flat. Tear napkins into odd-shaped pieces. (Any size pieces will work, but for a small vase, tear napkins into small pieces.)

2 Since all decoration is done from inside of vase, begin by positioning flowers (or sunburst motifs) first for best effect. Working over a small area at a time, brush a coat of glue on inside of vase. Press flower petals (or sunburst motifs) right side down into glue, 1 at a time. Brush glue between layers of petals to hold them together. In same manner, press leaves into glue. Coat flowers, leaves (or motifs), and surrounding surface with glue. Press paper napkin pieces into glue, covering flowers, leaves (or motifs), and uncovered areas of vase. Brush a coat of glue over napkin pieces. Continue gluing flowers, leaves (or motifs), and napkin pieces to vase until desired effect is achieved. Let dry. (Drying can take several days due to the thickness of the silk flowers.)

3 If desired, eliminate slight stickiness of decorated surface by applying 1 coat of finish. Let dry.

Quick Decoupage

Paper cutouts are easy to collect. Save your favorites to create a personal display of decoupaged projects.

Use a small suitcase to add a touch of whimsy to your den. This case is decoupaged with motifs cut from theme gift wrap paper and other travel-related papers. For a child's toy case, use playful papers perhaps depicting cars or dolls.

Materials (for all items shown)

For each: ½" shader paintbrush
Sponge paintbrush
Aleene's Instant Decoupage Glue and Finish™
Paper items for decoration: doilies, gift wrap cutouts, greeting card cutouts, or other decorative paper items
Aleene's Right-On Finish™ (optional)
For tray: Oval wooden tray
Fine-grade sandpaper
Cream acrylic paint
For suitcase: Small suitcase
Newspaper
Aleene's Tacky Glue™
Burnt sienna acrylic paint
For box: Round papier-mâché box
Blue acrylic paint

Directions

1 **To prepare tray for decoration,** thoroughly sand all surfaces to remove any rough edges or imperfections. Base piece needs to have a smooth and even surface. (*Hint:* "Many pieces are labeled as presanded, but I have found that the pieces still need a bit of sanding before painting," says Heidi.)

2 **To prepare suitcase for decoration,** tear or cut newspaper into 1" to 2" squares. Working with 1 small area at a time, brush a coat of Tacky Glue on suitcase. Place 1 square of newspaper over glued area and brush another coat of Tacky Glue over newspaper. Continue in same manner, overlapping edges of newspaper slightly, until entire surface is covered. Let dry.

3 Using paintbrush, paint base piece (**tray, newspaper-covered suitcase, or box**) with 1 or more coats of acrylic paint, letting paint dry between applications. If surface feels rough or uneven after painting, lightly sand and apply another coat of paint. Let dry. Using sponge brush, apply 1 coat of Decoupage Glue to entire surface and let dry.

4 Cut out desired motifs from gift wrap, greeting cards, or other decorative papers. Arrange cutouts on base piece to determine placement. (Remember that layering cutouts and doilies adds interest and texture.) Remove paper pieces from base piece. To apply 1 paper piece to base piece, use sponge brush to apply a coat of Decoupage Glue to base piece in desired position. Place paper piece on glue-covered area and use fingers to press out any air bubbles. Brush a coat of Decoupage Glue on top of paper piece, covering edges of paper. In same manner, apply additional paper pieces to base piece until desired effect is achieved. Let dry.

5 If desired, apply 1 coat of finish to entire surface of piece to protect decoupage from wear and tear. Let dry.

Flower Garland

Sponge-paint simple brown bag flowers to create this unusual floral garland. You'll be surprised at the many ways you can use a garland to decorate your home.

Materials

Patterns on page 32
Brown grocery bags
3" square cardboard for squeegee
Aleene's Tacky Glue™
Acrylic paints: black, yellow, brown, purple, pink, teal, medium green, light green
Paintbrush
Small sponge pieces
Clothespins
Florist's wire: 1 (6") length 22-gauge for each flower and leaf, 38" length 18-gauge for garland
Pinking shears
Green florist's tape

Directions

Note: See page 139 for tips on sponge painting. The 38"-long garland shown here has 9 flowers and 16 leaves. You can make garland longer or shorter than 38" by adjusting length of 18-gauge florist's wire. Don't forget to adjust number of flowers and leaves as well.

1 **For each flower,** cut 2 (6") squares of brown bag. Using cardboard squeegee, apply 1 coat of glue to 1 side of 1 brown bag piece. With edges aligned, press remaining brown bag piece into glue. Transfer patterns to layered bag and cut 1 flower and 1 flower center. Cut slit in flower as indicated on pattern. Let dry. Brush a coat of

black paint on flower and flower center. Let dry. Sponge-paint flower center with yellow and brown, letting dry between colors. Sponge-paint flower with purple, pink, and teal, letting dry between colors.

2 **To assemble each flower,** overlap edges of slit, aligning petal edges, and glue to secure. Hold petals in place with clothespin until glue is dry. For stem, curve 1" of 1 end of 1 (6") wire into a spiral. Push straight end of wire through center of flower from right side until spiral is flush with flower. Glue spiral to flower to secure. Apply glue to wrong side of flower center. Press flower center onto flower, covering wire spiral. Press a pencil eraser on edges of flower center to shape as desired. Let dry. Repeat steps 1 and 2 to make 8 more flowers.

3 **For each leaf,** cut 2 (2" x 4") pieces of brown bag. Transfer pattern to 1 brown bag piece. With edges aligned, pattern side up, and 1 (6") wire sandwiched between as indicated on pattern, glue bag pieces together, using cardboard squeegee to apply 1 coat of glue between bag layers. Cut out leaf, using pinking shears to cut pointed end (see photo); do not cut through wire. Let dry. Brush a coat of black paint on leaf. Let dry. Sponge-paint leaf with medium green and light green, letting dry between colors. Repeat to make 15 more leaves.

4 **To assemble garland,** using florist's tape, wrap stems and attach flowers and leaves to 18-gauge florist's wire, covering 2" of free end of each stem and arranging flowers and leaves as desired. (Remember that florist's tape must be stretched as it is wrapped so that it will stick to itself.) Shape garland as desired.

Accent Your Home with Simple Flowers

The sponge-painted finish on these brown bag flowers looks like verdigris. So instead of purchasing an expensive copper garland in a fancy store, you can create your own from ordinary grocery bags. Below are just a few ways to use this garland in your home.

• Use as a tieback for curtains.
• Wrap around the baluster of a floor lamp.
• Twine around the banisters of a staircase.
• Wrap around a natural vine wreath.
• Drape across the top of a window or a door.
• Make an arrangement for a mantel.
• Drape across the top of a hutch or an armoire.
• Twist the ends of the garland together to make a small wreath for your foyer.

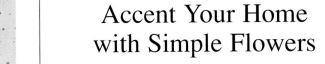

Celestial Pillows

Heavenly motifs make these pillows
a great addition to your living room.

Materials (for both)

For each: Aleene's Fusible Web™
Aleene's OK to Wash-It™ Glue
Thread to match fabrics and needle (optional)
14" square pillow form
Batting
For star pillow: Pattern on page 32
Fabric: 16" x 38" piece black star print, 12" square
    white celestial print
Gold glitter dimensional paint
For charms pillow: 16" x 38" piece white star print
70" length ¼"-diameter white-and-gold metallic
    cording
7" x 24" piece gold lace
Assorted moon and star charms

Directions

Note: See page 136 for tips on working with
fusible web.

1 **For each pillow cover,** wash and dry fabric;
do not use fabric softener in washer or dryer.
Fuse 1"-wide strips of fusible web to each 16"
edge on wrong side of star print fabric. Turn under
1" at each 16" edge and fuse for hem. With right
sides facing, fold hemmed ends of fabric toward
middle, overlapping hemmed ends 8" and making
a 14" x 16" piece. Glue or stitch side edges together using a 1" seam. Let glue dry. Turn pillow cover
right side out.

2 **For star pillow,** iron fusible web to wrong
side of celestial print fabric. Transfer star pattern to paper side of web and cut out. Center star
on pillow cover front and fuse. Embellish star and
pillow cover front with dots of dimensional paint
as desired. Let dry.

3 **For each pillow,** wrap pillow form with 1
layer of batting and insert into pillow cover.

4 **For charms pillow,** wrap and knot cording
around pillow. Tie gold lace in a bow around
center of cording. Glue or stitch charms to pillow
cover front as desired. Let dry.

Purchased Pillow Dress-ups

Add a quick, fancy touch to plain throw pillows by whipping up a bow or a flower band. Very inexpensive pillows can be transformed into decorator accents with just a bit of fabric.

Materials (for both)

For each: 14" square throw pillow
Aleene's Fusible Web™
Aleene's OK to Wash-It™ Glue
For bow: Print fabric to match pillow: 9" x 29" strip for pillow band, 5" x 5½" piece for bow center, 12½" x 19" piece for bow
Batting
For flower: Print fabric to match pillow: 8" x 29" strip for pillow band, 2 (7" x 8") pieces for leaves, 6" x 29" piece for flower
Clothespins

Directions

Note: See page 136 for tips on working with fusible web.

1 **To make each pillow band,** fuse a 1"-wide strip of fusible web along 1 (29") edge on wrong side of fabric strip. Fold over both long edges of strip, overlapping edges 1", and fuse to make a tube. Glue short raw ends together, overlapping ends 2", to form a circle. Pin ends together until glue is dry.

2 **For bow pillow,** to make bow center, fuse a 1"-wide strip of fusible web along 1 (5½") edge on wrong side of bow center piece. Fold over both 5½" edges of fabric, overlapping edges 1", and fuse to make a tube. Set aside.

3 To make bow, fuse a 1"-wide strip of fusible web along 1 (19") edge on wrong side of bow piece. Fold over both long edges of fabric, overlapping edges 1", and fuse to make a tube. Lay fabric tube flat on work surface and measure width and length. Subtract 2" from length measurement and cut 1 piece of batting to fit. Put batting inside tube, leaving 1" of fabric at each end. Cut 2 (1"-wide) strips of fusible web to fit open ends of tube. Turn ½" around each open end to inside of tube. Insert 1 strip of web in each end and fuse to close.

4 To assemble bow, pinch center of bow to gather. Wrap bow center, seam side down, around gathered bow, overlapping ends 1". Glue bow center ends together. Pin ends together until glue is dry. Referring to photo, glue bow to pillow band, covering glued ends of band. Pin bow to band until glue is dry. Slip band around pillow.

5 **For flower pillow,** to make each leaf, fuse a 1"-wide strip of fusible web along 1 (8") edge on wrong side of leaf piece. Fold over both long edges of fabric, overlapping edges 1", and fuse to make a tube. Lay tube, seam side up, on work surface. Referring to *Leaf Diagram,* fold down ends of tube to form leaf. Gather raw ends of tube and glue together. Pin gathered ends together until glue is dry.

Leaf Diagram

6 To make flower, squeeze a thin line of glue along each short end on wrong side of flower piece. Turn under ½" along each short end and press into glue. Let dry for a few minutes. Squeeze a thin line of glue along 1 (29") edge on wrong side of fabric. With wrong sides facing, fold fabric in half lengthwise and press together along glue line. Let dry for a few minutes. Squeeze a thin line of glue along glued 29" edge of folded fabric. (*Hint:* Use glue sparingly to make fabric easier to roll when forming flower.)

Referring to *Flower Diagram* and beginning at 1 end of folded strip, roll folded fabric, gathering bottom edge of fabric and pinching fabric together to form flower. Use pins and clothespins to hold gathered edge of flower together until glue is dry. Referring to photo, glue leaves and flower to pillow band, covering glued ends of band. Pin leaves and flowers to band until glue is dry. Slip band around pillow.

Flower Diagram

Seasonal Flags

Flags are adorning homes across the country. Mark the changing seasons with spring and autumn flags shown here and on the next page.

Materials (for both)

For each: Aleene's Fusible Web™
26" length ⅜"-diameter wooden dowel
2 (1¼"-diameter) wooden balls, each with ⅜"-diameter hole
Paintbrush
Aleene's Professional Wood Glue™
For spring flag: Patterns on page 33
Fabric: 24" x 49" piece white polished cotton for flag; 18" square green for pansy leaves; 1 (16" x 24") piece each pink, light purple, and dark purple for petals
Dimensional paints: black, yellow
White acrylic paint
For autumn flag: Patterns on page 34
Fabric: 26" x 46" piece white-on-white leaf print for flag, 7 (11") squares assorted brown prints for autumn leaves and pumpkin stem, 8" x 10" piece orange minidot for pumpkin
Dimensional paints: gold glitter, dark green
Brown acrylic paint

Directions

Note: See page 136 for tips on working with fusible web.

1 **For each flag,** wash and dry fabric; do not use fabric softener in washer or dryer. Fuse 1"-wide strips of fusible web to each edge on wrong side of flag fabric. To hem flag, turn under 1" along both long sides and 1 short end and fuse. To make dowel casing, turn under 4" along remaining short end of fabric and fuse.

2 Iron fusible web to wrong side of remaining fabrics. **For spring flag,** transfer patterns to paper side of web and cut 5 green pansy leaves, 5 pink petals, 5 light purple petals, and 5 dark purple

continued on page 20

petals. Referring to photo and *Pansy Diagram,* fuse leaves and petals to flag. Referring to photo, embellish leaves and pansies with dimensional paints. Let dry. **For autumn flag,** transfer patterns to paper side of web and cut 7 brown print autumn leaves, 1 brown print stem, and 1 orange minidot pumpkin. Referring to photo, fuse leaves, pumpkin, and stem to flag. Referring to photo, embellish leaves and pumpkin with dimensional paint. Paint pine boughs with dimensional paints. Let dry.

3 **For each flag,** paint dowel and wooden balls with acrylic paint. Let dry. Slip dowel

through casing in flag. Glue 1 wooden ball to each end of dowel. Let dry.

Pansy Diagram

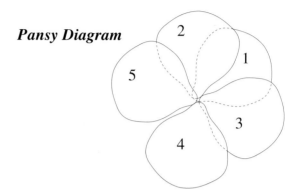

Candle Holders

Add romance to your table with a group of votive candles. Cast soft, glowing candlelight on any occasion with these designs.

Materials (for 1 candle holder)
Patterns on pages 35 and 36
Brown grocery bags
3" square cardboard for squeegee
Aleene's Tacky Glue™
Votive candle and glass holder
Rubber band
Acrylic paints: green, purple, pink, teal, yellow, orange
Small sponge pieces

Directions
Note: See page 139 for tips on sponge painting.

1 **For each candle holder,** cut 4 (9") squares of brown bag. With edges aligned, glue brown bag squares together, applying 1 coat of glue between layers, using cardboard squeegee.

2 **For tulip candle holder,** transfer candle holder pattern to layered bag and cut out. Fold candle holder along fold lines as indicated on pattern. Place glass candle holder inside bag holder and glue tulip petals together where they touch. Place rubber band around holder until glue is dry. Remove glass holder from bag holder. **For geometric candle holder,** transfer patterns to layered bag and cut 1 candle holder, 4 circles, 4 half circles, and 4 triangles. Fold candle holder along fold lines as indicated on pattern.

3 **For each candle holder,** spread a fairly thick coat of glue on right side of each piece using fingers. Refer to Burnt Brown Bag How-to on pages 138 and 139 to burn each piece.

4 **For tulip candle holder,** sponge-paint leaves with green. Sponge-paint 2 tulips with purple and pink, letting dry between colors. Sponge-paint remaining 2 tulips with teal and purple, letting dry between colors.

5 **For geometric candle holder,** sponge-paint holder and each triangle with green, teal, purple, and pink, letting dry between colors. Sponge-paint circles with yellow and orange, letting dry between colors. Sponge-paint half circles with purple and pink, letting dry between colors.

6 **To assemble geometric candle holder,** glue 1 triangle to back of each rectangle. Referring to photo, glue 1 circle to front of each triangle at tip and 1 half circle to front of each rectangle at bottom. Glue glass candle holder inside bag holder. Place rubber band around holder until glue is dry.

Decorated Lamps & Shades

A purchased kit allows you to customize lighting for your home. Use left-over upholstery or drapery fabric for a coordinated look. Or create a unique theme lamp like the yarn-and-buttons one shown here.

Materials (for both)

For each: Aleene's Designer Tacky Glue™

For pansy lamp: Self-adhesive Brass Dec-A-Lamp kit by Northland Designs*

Fabric: 7" x 13" piece white pansy print for base, ½ yard 45"-wide black pansy print for shade

Silk pansies and leaves

Tiny dried flowers

Ribbon: 1 yard 1⅜"-wide silk organdy, 1 yard ⅛"-wide purple satin

4" length 26-gauge florist's wire

For yarn-and-buttons lamp: Self-adhesive Spool Dec-A-Lamp kit and Self-adhesive Design-A-Shade kit by Northland Designs*

Acrylic paints: cream, silver

Paintbrush

1 skein blue 4-ply acrylic yarn

9¼" length ⅛"-diameter wooden dowel

Craft knife

Fine-tip permanent black marker

½ yard 45"-wide blue flower print fabric

1 yard 1½"-wide pregathered lace trim

Assorted buttons

Directions

* Check your local crafts or hobby store for lamp kits by Northland Designs. For more information about these lamp kits, write to Northland Designs, 800 Wisconsin Avenue, Suite D02-100, Eau Claire WI 54701, or call them at (715) 834-8707.

1 **For pansy lamp,** referring to manufacturer's directions, cover lamp base with white pansy print fabric. Cover shade with black pansy print fabric, leaving ¼" of fabric at top and bottom of shade. Turn excess fabric to inside of shade and glue, clipping curves as needed. Let dry.

2 Referring to photo, glue silk pansies and dried flowers to base. Let dry. Make 4" loops in organdy ribbon and arrange in a fan shape. Glue ribbon loops together and glue to shade. Let dry. Glue silk pansies and dried flowers on top of ribbon and let dry. Make a multilooped bow with purple ribbon, using florist's wire to secure bow. Glue bow to shade below flowers (see photo). Let dry.

3 **For yarn-and-buttons lamp,** referring to manufacturer's directions, paint top and bottom of spool cream. Let dry. Wrap yarn around adhesive area of lamp base to cover. For needle, using craft knife, shape 1 end of dowel to a point and flatten other end for eye of needle. Paint dowel needle silver and let dry. Draw eye on needle with black marker. Cut 1 (16") length and 1 (18") length of yarn. Glue 1 end of each length to opposite sides of needle at eye. Let dry. Referring to photo, push needle through yarn on lamp.

4 Cover shade with flower print fabric, leaving ¼" of fabric at top and bottom of shade. Turn excess fabric to inside of shade and glue, clipping curves as needed. Let dry. Glue lace trim around top and bottom edges of shade, overlapping trim ends ½". Let dry. Referring to photo, glue buttons to shade. Let dry.

Sunny Setting

Greet the start of each day with a bright, flowery place setting on your breakfast table.

Materials (for 1 set)

Pattern on page 36
Denim place mat
Disappearing-ink pen
Yellow dimensional paint
Orange crystal-glitter brush-on paint
Paintbrush
Blue chambray fabric: 14" square for napkin,
   2⅜" x 6½" piece for napkin ring
Aleene's OK to Wash-It™ Glue
Yellow rickrack: 2 (14") lengths for napkin,
   6¼" length for napkin ring
1⅛"-long piece toilet tissue tube
1 small silk sunflower with leaves

Directions

1 **For mat,** center and draw a circle about 10" in diameter on place mat using disappearing-ink pen. (*Hint:* A dinner plate is the perfect size for this circle.) Transferring petal pattern to mat using disappearing-ink pen, draw petals around marked circle as desired. Apply yellow dimensional paint to all marked lines. Let dry. Paint each petal with orange crystal-glitter paint. Let dry.

2 **For napkin,** turn under ¼" along each edge of chambray square and glue for hem. Let dry. Positioning rickrack 1¼" from 1 hemmed edge of napkin and leaving ¼" free at each end, glue 1 (14") length of rickrack to right side of napkin. Let dry. Turn under ¼" at each end of rickrack and glue. Let dry. Repeat to glue remaining 14" length of rickrack to opposite edge of napkin.

3 **For napkin ring,** spread glue on outside of toilet tissue ring. Cover ring with 2⅜" x 6½" chambray piece, overlapping ends. Spread glue on inside of ring. Fold excess fabric to inside of ring, overlapping edges. Let dry. Center and glue 6¼" length of rickrack around outside of ring. Let dry. Glue sunflower and leaves to ring, covering ends of fabric and rickrack. Pin until glue is dry.

Burnt Brown Bag Wind Chimes

The soothing sound of wind chimes can be yours with this unusual owl design. Gold paste paint highlights the textural surface of the burnt brown bag piece.

Materials

Patterns on page 37
Brown grocery bags
3" square cardboard for squeegee
Aleene's Tacky Glue™
20" length 22-gauge florist's wire
Black acrylic paint
Paintbrush
Gold paste paint
Aleene's Designer Tacky Glue™
Ice pick
5 (2"-diameter) metal washers
Drill with 1/16"-diameter bit
11" length 1"-diameter tree branch
20-pound test fishing line

Directions

1 Cut 2 (7" x 11") pieces of brown bag. Using cardboard squeegee, apply 1 coat of Tacky Glue to 1 side of 1 brown bag piece. With edges aligned, press remaining 7" x 11" brown bag piece into glue. Transfer patterns to layered bag and cut 1 ears, 1 feet, 1 eyes, 2 pupils, and 2 wings. Cut slits in each wing as indicated on pattern. Fold ears piece along line indicated on pattern. Fold eyes piece along line indicated on pattern to shape beak. Transfer body pattern to remaining brown bag twice and cut out. With edges aligned and wire sandwiched between as indicated on pattern, glue body pieces together, using cardboard squeegee to apply 1 coat of Tacky Glue between layers.

2 Spread a fairly thick coat of Tacky Glue on both sides of each piece using fingers. Refer to Burnt Brown Bag How-to on pages 138 and 139 to burn each piece. Let dry.

3 Paint pupils black. Let dry. To add gold highlights to remaining pieces, rub finger in gold paste paint, wipe off excess on paper towel, and gently rub finger over each burned piece. Continue adding gold to each piece, except pupils, until desired effect is achieved. Let dry.

4 Referring to photo, shape body piece to form an oval 6" tall and 4" wide. Using Designer Tacky Glue, glue pieces together to make owl (see photo). Let dry. Using ice pick, center and poke 1 hole through top of owl for hanger.

5 Paint washers black and let dry. Highlight washers with gold as in Step 3 and let dry.

6 Drill 5 holes side by side through center of tree branch. Also drill 1 hole through branch about ½" from each end. Cut 5 (20" to 22") lengths of fishing line. Tie 1 washer to 1 end of each length of fishing line. Thread other end of lengths through holes in center of tree branch and knot. (Be sure washers will touch when hanging.) Cut 1 (50") length of fishing line for hanger. Thread 1 end of fishing line through each hole at ends of branch and knot. Thread center of hanger up through hole in owl. Measure down from top of hanger loop to top of owl. Remove loop from owl and knot hanger loop at that measurement. Thread loop back up through hole in owl so that knot fits snugly inside top of owl. Place dots of Designer Tacky Glue on all knots to secure. Let dry.

Bread Dough Rose Frame

Adjust the number of bread dough roses to match the openings in your chosen collage frame.

Materials

14" x 16" piece ivory lace
11½" x 14½" frame and collage mat with 7 openings
Aleene's Tacky Glue™
7 (12") lengths 1/16"-wide ivory satin ribbon
7 (3") lengths 26-gauge florist's wire
Bread dough: 1 small ball each light green, yellow, pink, and mauve; 2 yellow, 2 blue, and 3 mauve roses; 34 light green leaves in assorted sizes

Directions

Note: Refer to pages 140–142 for bread dough recipe as well as bread dough rose and leaf how-tos.

1 Place lace right side down on work surface. Center mat right side down on lace. Fold excess lace to back of mat and glue, being sure lace is taut. Let dry. Cut openings in lace, leaving ¼" of lace around inside of each mat opening. Fold excess lace to back of mat and glue, clipping curves as needed and being sure lace is taut. Let dry.

2 For each opening, make a multilooped bow with 1 ribbon length, using 1 length of florist's wire to secure bow. Glue 1 bow to mat above each opening. Let dry.

3 For each bread dough vine, pinch off a seed bead-sized piece of light green bread dough. Roll dough between hands into a thin snake shape. Shape vine as desired. Repeat to make 7 more vine pieces. For tiny bead flowers, pinch off a seed bead-sized piece of yellow dough and roll between hands to form a ball. Repeat to make additional yellow, pink, and mauve tiny bead flowers. Referring to photo, glue bread dough pieces to mat. Let dry.

Fancy Frames

A pretty picture frame will enhance your favorite photo while adding a decorative touch to your home. Choose from these three quick-and-easy ideas to decorate frames for your treasured snapshots.

Tropical Frame

It's easy to dress up a frame for your beach pictures. Simply glue batting to one side of a picture mat and trim the batting from the mat opening. Referring to Step 1 of the Bread Dough Rose Frame on page 28, cover the padded side of the mat with a piece of tropical print fabric. Sponge-paint a wooden frame with colors to match the print fabric and let the paint dry. (See page 139 for tips on sponge painting.) Insert the fabric-covered mat into the frame. Glue a raffia bow and an assortment of seashells to the mat, using Aleene's Designer Tacky Glue.

Heidi's Hint

Use this same idea to create themed picture frames to give as gifts. For a new mother, cover the mat with a baby motif fabric and then glue on tiny baby shoes, a baby bottle, or other miniature items. Select a sports motif fabric and collect miniatures suited to your child's team. Crafts stores, hobby stores, and party goods stores are excellent places to find miniatures to carry out your chosen theme. Be sure to check the cake decorating section of the store, because miniature items are often used to decorate birthday cakes or cupcakes.

Beaded Frames

Glue assorted buttons, beads, and charms to a frame as desired, using Aleene's Designer Tacky Glue. A broken necklace or loose pieces of costume jewelry are ideal sources for items to decorate a frame. Buy charms or special beads on sale at your local crafts store to create a one-of-a-kind frame. (Also watch for discounts on frames in crafts and variety stores.)

Acrylic Box Frame

Squeegee a very thin layer of Aleene's Tacky Glue on the cardboard insert that comes with an acrylic box frame. Cover the cardboard with gift wrap, being sure to press out any air bubbles. Let the glue dry. Cut decorative motifs from the gift wrap as desired. Squeegee glue on the wrong side of each motif and glue them to the front of the acrylic frame as desired. Let the glue dry. Center a picture on the gift wrap-covered cardboard insert and place it in the frame.

31

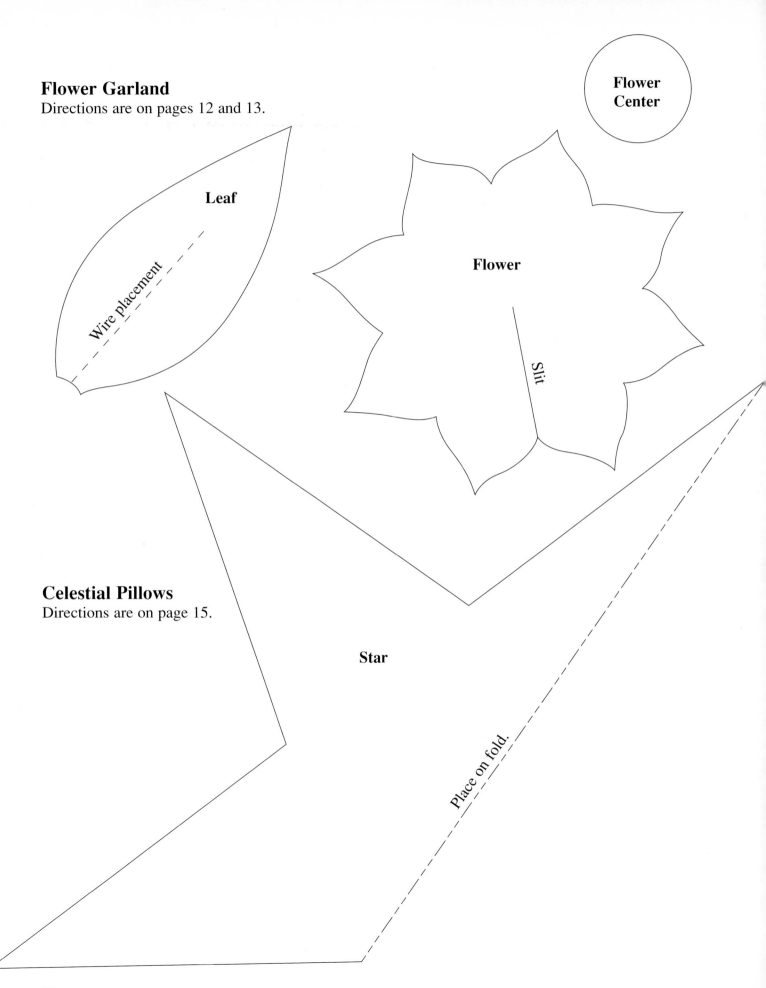

Flower Garland
Directions are on pages 12 and 13.

Leaf

Wire placement

Flower
Center

Flower

Slit

Celestial Pillows
Directions are on page 15.

Star

Place on fold.

Seasonal Flags
Directions are on pages 18–20.

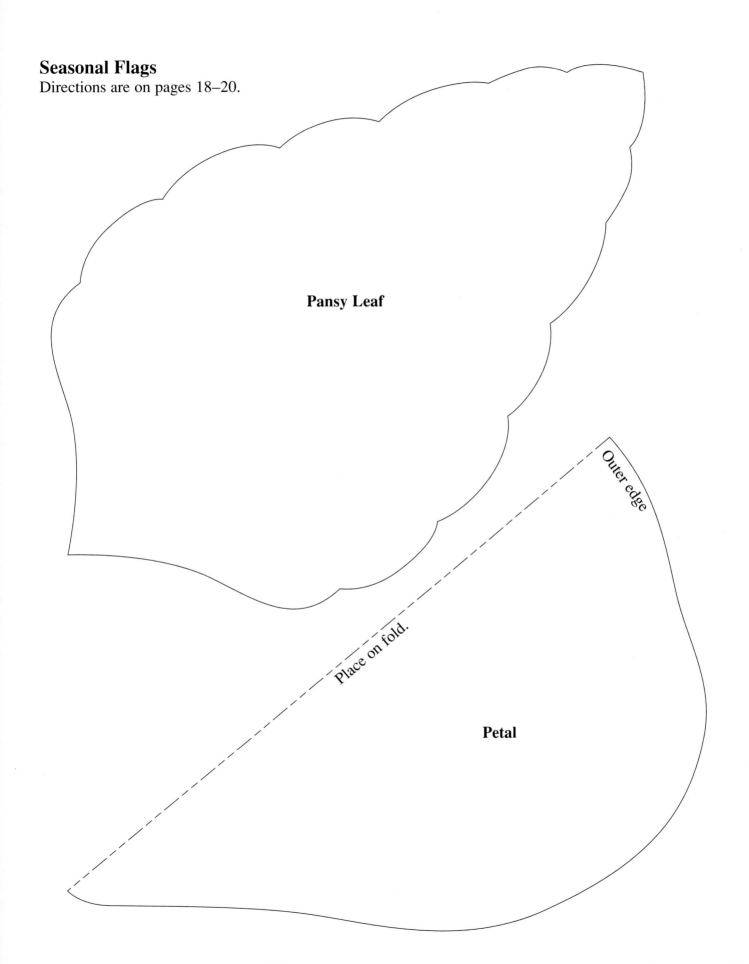

Pansy Leaf

Outer edge

Place on fold.

Petal

Seasonal Flags
Directions are on pages 18–20.

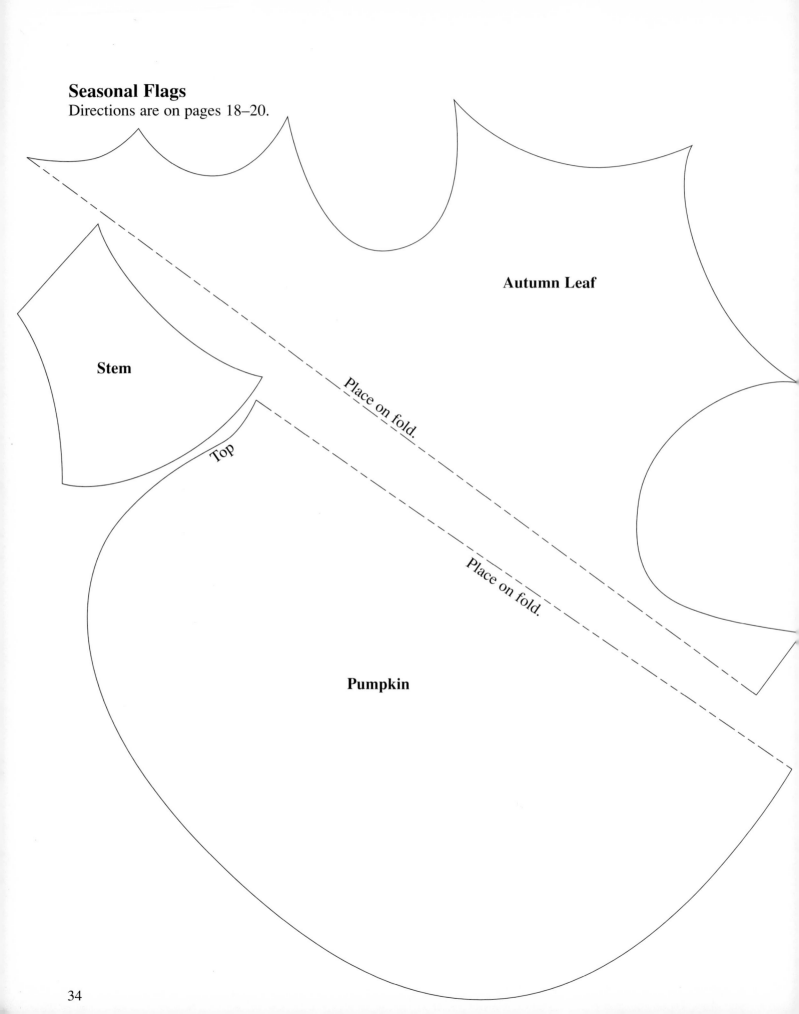

Autumn Leaf

Stem

Top

Place on fold.

Place on fold.

Pumpkin

Candle Holders

Directions are on page 21.

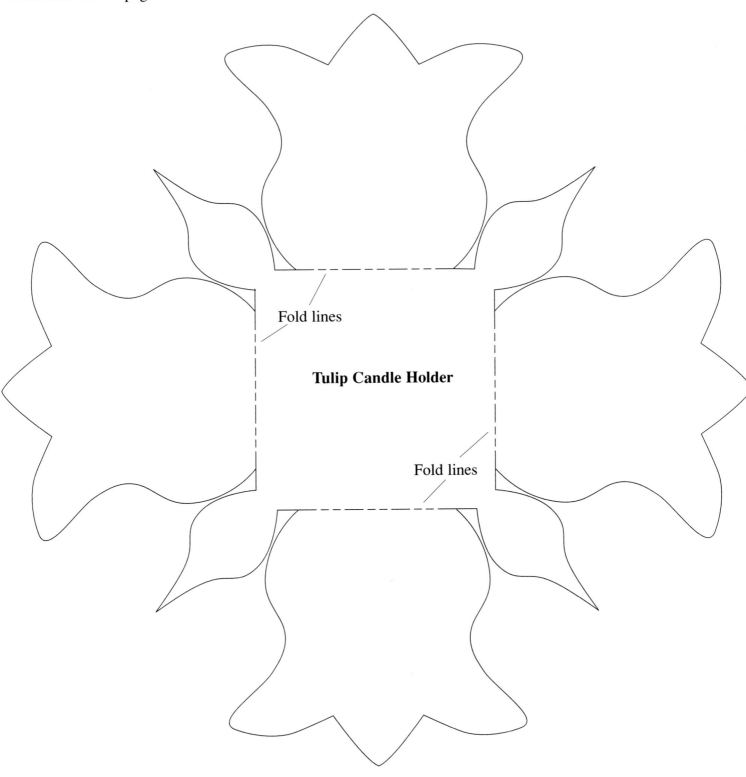

Fold lines

Tulip Candle Holder

Fold lines

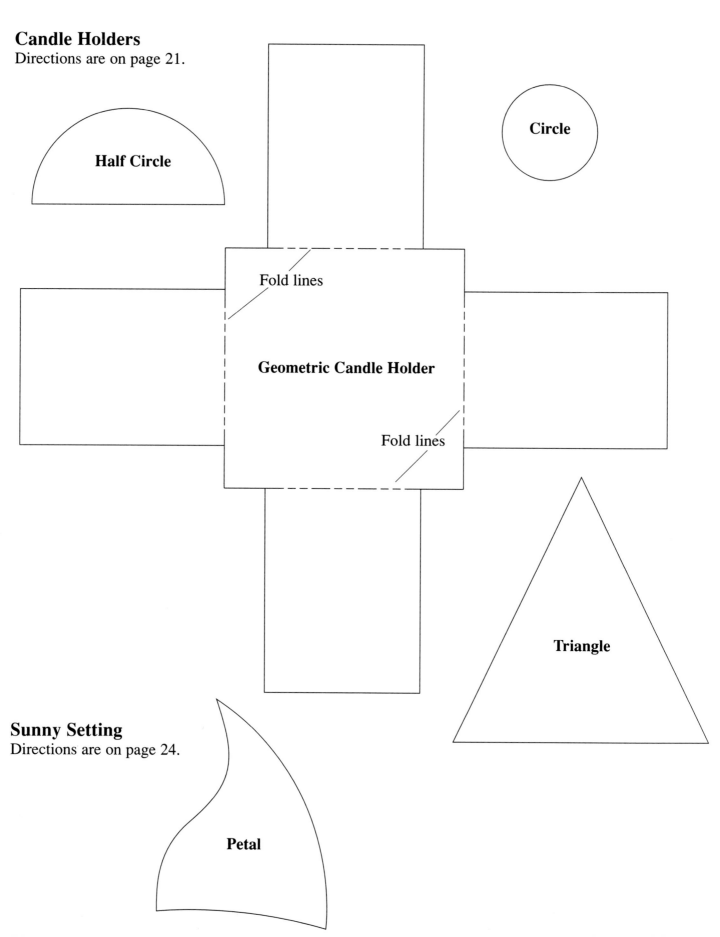

Candle Holders
Directions are on page 21.

Half Circle

Circle

Fold lines

Geometric Candle Holder

Fold lines

Triangle

Sunny Setting
Directions are on page 24.

Petal

Burnt Brown Bag Wind Chimes

Directions are on page 27.

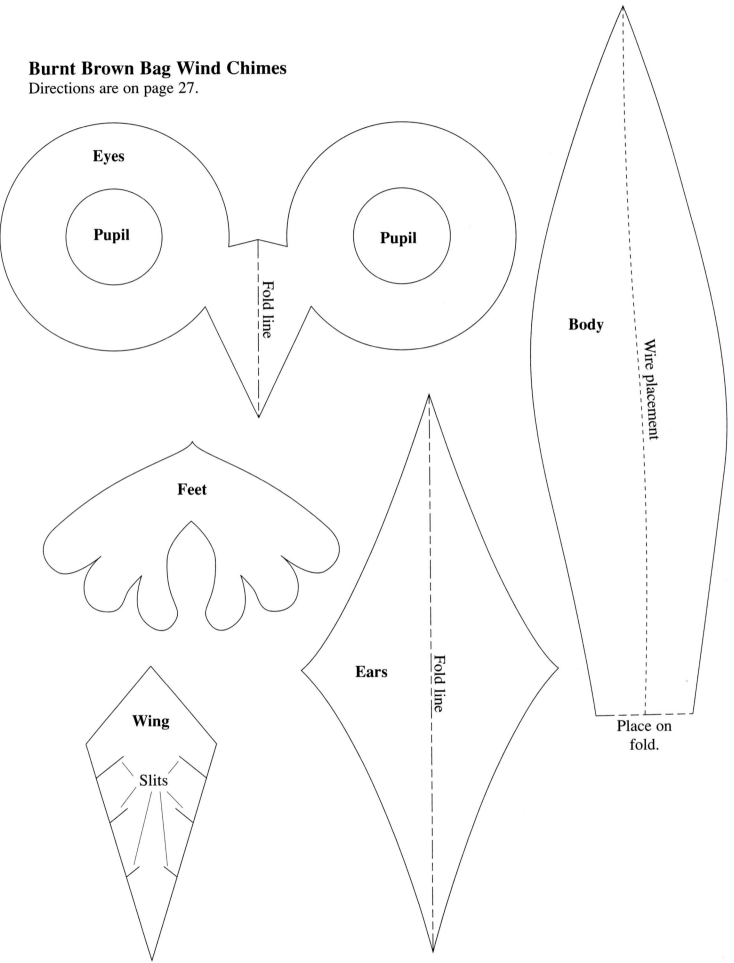

Eyes

Pupil

Pupil

Fold line

Body

Wire placement

Feet

Ears

Fold line

Place on fold.

Wing

Slits

Fun with Fashion

Don't spend a fortune on your new wardrobe. Look through the following pages to craft one-of-a-kind garments. You'll find a jacket stenciled with glittery fish and a simple black dress sponge-painted with stars.

39

Paper Napkin Appliqué

Paper napkins are an easy way to decorate wearables. Believe it or not, the glue makes the napkin cutouts washable. Just be sure to completely seal the cutouts with glue.

Materials (for both)
White shirt
Cardboard covered with waxed paper
Straw hat
White spray paint
Flower motif paper napkins
Disappearing-ink pen
Paintbrush
Aleene's Paper Napkin Appliqué™ Glue
White pearlescent dimensional paint

Directions

1 Wash and dry shirt; do not use fabric softener in washer or dryer. Place cardboard covered with waxed paper inside shirt. Spray-paint hat white. Let dry.

2 Cut motifs from napkins as desired. Cut some flowers with leaves and some individual blossoms. (Don't worry about being too precise when cutting out motifs.) Remove bottom plies of napkin to leave cutouts 1 ply thick.

3 For shirt, place 1 napkin cutout on shirt front as desired. Using disappearing-ink pen, lightly trace around cutout. Remove cutout. Brush an even coat of glue on shirt front inside traced line. Place cutout on glue-covered area and press out air bubbles. Gently brush top of cutout with a coat of glue. (Glue has a pale blue tint when wet but will dry clear.) Repeat to apply additional napkin cutouts to shirt front, collar, and button placket (see photo). Let dry.

4 For hat, brush an even coat of glue on hat in desired position. Place 1 napkin cutout in glue-covered area and press out air bubbles. Gently brush top of cutout with a coat of glue. Repeat to apply additional napkin cutouts to hat as desired. Let dry.

5 For shirt and hat, outline and embellish napkin cutouts with dimensional paint. Let dry.

6 Do not wash shirt for at least 1 week. Turn shirt wrong side out, wash by hand, and hang to dry.

Heidi's Hint

Be sure to completely seal the napkin cutouts between two coats of glue (one on the item being decorated and one on top of the cutout). If you do not completely sandwich the cutouts between two coats of glue, the napkin cutouts will come off during washing. The glue seals the napkin cutouts and bonds them to the wearable.

Fancy Vests

Glue bows and charms to a black quilted vest for stunning evening wear. For a dressed-up denim vest, apply lace and gold braided trim.

Materials (for both)
For each: Aleene's Jewel-It™ Glue
Cardboard covered with waxed paper
For beribboned vest: Black vest
10" to 12" lengths assorted ribbons
Assorted gold bow charms
For braid-and-lace vest: Denim vest
2 (4" x 11") pieces black lace
Assorted gold-and-black braided trims
Aleene's Shrink-It™ Plastic scraps
Clothespins

Directions

1 **For each,** wash and dry vest; do not use fabric softener in washer or dryer. Place cardboard covered with waxed paper inside vest.

2 **For beribboned vest,** tie each ribbon length in a bow. Referring to photo, glue bows and charms on vest. Pin bows in place until glue is dry.

3 **For braid-and-lace vest,** cut lace to desired shape and size; glue in place on vest. Referring to photo, glue braided trims to vest. Pin trims in place until glue is dry. To glue trim over edges at armholes, turn ¾" to 1" of trim to wrong side of vest and glue. Sandwich glued areas between scraps of Shrink-It and secure with a clothespin until glue is dry. (If desired, glue a length of gold braided trim around neck of a black T-shirt for a complete ensemble.)

4 Do not wash vest for at least 2 weeks. Turn vest wrong side out, wash by hand, and hang to dry.

Rose Button Covers & Pin

The tiny ribbon fans and delicate roses in this set are reminiscent of Victorian finery. The bread dough roses look like fine porcelain.

Materials (for 1 set)
1"-wide ecru satin ribbon: 3½" length, 5 (2½") lengths
Aleene's Designer Tacky Glue™
Ecru thread and needle
½" x 1" piece cardboard
Clothespin
Pearl string: 5¼" length, 5 (3¾") lengths
Bread dough: 6 pink roses, 1 pink rosebud with calyx and 1 leaf, 17 medium green leaves
Pin back
5 metal button covers

Directions
Note: Refer to pages 140–142 for bread dough recipe as well as bread dough rose and leaf how-tos.

1 To make ribbon fan for pin, turn under ⅛" at each short end of 3½" ribbon length and glue. Let dry. Using needle and thread, run a gathering thread along 1 long edge of ribbon. Pull to gather and secure thread. In same manner, make 1 ribbon fan for each button cover, using 2½" ribbon lengths.

2 For pin, with gathered end of ribbon fan at top, glue cardboard to back of ribbon fan. Use clothespin to hold until glue is dry. Referring to photo, loop 5¼" length of pearl string and glue to ribbon fan. Let dry. Glue 1 bread dough rose, 1 bread dough rosebud with calyx and leaf, and 2 bread dough leaves to ribbon fan on top of pearl string. Let dry. Glue pin back to back of cardboard. Let dry.

3 For each button cover, with gathered end of ribbon fan at top, glue 1 button cover to back of 1 ribbon fan. Use clothespin to hold until glue is dry. Referring to photo, loop 1 (3¾") length of pearl string and glue to ribbon fan. Let dry. Glue 1 bread dough rose and 3 bread dough leaves to ribbon fan on top of pearl string. Let dry.

Window Screen Jewelry

Cut stars from metal window screen and then coat the sharp edges with glue and the soft sheen of metallic paints. These pieces of jewelry are surprisingly lightweight.

Materials (for 1 necklace and 2 earrings)

Patterns on page 62
Aleene's Tacky Glue™
12" square metal window screen
Wire cutters
Metallic acrylic paints: silver, gold, copper
Paintbrush
Needlenose pliers
20 gold jump rings
9 size-12 brass snap swivels
17 size-10 brass snap swivels
2 size-7 brass snap swivels
2 fishhook earrings

Directions

Note: Brass snap swivels are available wherever fishing tackle is sold.

1 Transferring patterns using glue, draw 6 large stars and 14 small stars on window screen. Let dry. Using wire cutters, cut out stars. Apply additional glue to all edges of stars, being sure to cover all sharp points. Let dry. If any sharp points remain after glue dries, snip them off with wire cutters.

2 Paint both sides of each star, completely covering glue and allowing paint to fill some of the holes in the screen. For large stars, paint 2 silver, 2 gold, and 2 copper. For small stars, paint 5 silver, 5 gold, and 4 copper. Let dry.

3 Using needlenose pliers, attach 1 jump ring to top point of each star. For each earring, attach 1 small silver star to 1 size-12 snap, 1 small gold star to 1 size-10 snap, and 1 small copper star to 1 size-7 snap. Attach end of each swivel to 1 earring hook. For necklace, link together remaining swivel snaps, using size-12 snaps for back of necklace and size-10 snaps for front. Attach remaining 8 small stars and 6 large stars to necklace as desired.

Gardener's Delight

Have fun in the garden with this shirt and cap. Make matching jewelry (shown on next page) to wear to a casual backyard party.

Materials (for 1 outfit)

For shirt and hat: White T-shirt
Newspaper
Kraft paper
Cardboard covered with waxed paper
Spray bottle filled with water
Acrylic paints: yellow, orange, purple, red, green
Paintbrush
Dimensional paints: black, gold glitter
Letters ruler or guide (available in crafts or art supply stores)
6 flower seed packages
Waxed paper
Aleene's Transfer-It™
Aleene's OK to Wash-It™ Glue
White fabric painter's hat
For necklace and earrings: Pattern on page 62
Aleene's Opake Shrink-It™ Plastic
Fine-grade sandpaper
Fine-tip permanent black marker
Scalloped-edge scissors
Colored pencils
3⁄16"-diameter hole punch
Aleene's Baking Board or nonstick cookie sheet
Clear spray sealer
Needlenose pliers
1 gold jump ring
50" length black satin cording
32 pony beads in assorted colors
Aleene's Designer Tacky Glue™
2 earring backs

continued on page 48

Directions

1 **For T-shirt,** wash and dry T-shirt; do not use fabric softener in washer or dryer.

2 Cover work area with layers of newspaper. Cover layered newspaper with kraft paper to prevent newsprint from transferring to shirt. Place cardboard covered with waxed paper inside shirt. Spray shirt front with water until fabric is evenly coated. Brush paints on shirt front in desired position. (Water will cause paint to run. The more water in fabric, the more paint will run. If paint does not run as much as you would like, spray water over painted surface.) Repeat as desired. Drop dots of paint on shirt front as desired. Let dry.

3 Outline painted areas and add details with black dimensional paint. Let dry. Using letters ruler or guide and gold dimensional paint, add lettering to shirt (see photo). Let dry.

4 Remove seeds from packages. Cut out desired portion of each seed package. To prepare each seed package, lay cutout right side up on waxed paper. Brush a liberal, even coat of Transfer-It on right side of cutout. Let dry. Place cutout right side down on clean waxed paper. Spray wrong side of cutout with water until saturated. Working from center outward, carefully rub off paper with fingers. Blot with paper towel and let dry. (Image will be fairly transparent and will feel like a plastic bag.) Trim edges of cutout if necessary.

5 To apply each cutout to shirt, lay cutout right side down on clean waxed paper. Brush a coat of OK to Wash-It Glue on wrong side of cutout. Place cutout on shirt, glue side down, in desired position, pressing out any air bubbles. Let dry. Brush a coat of OK to Wash-It Glue on top of cutout, covering edges to seal. Let dry. Embellish cutouts with black dimensional paint as desired. Let dry.

6 Do not wash shirt for at least 1 week. Turn shirt wrong side out, wash by hand, and hang to dry.

7 **For hat,** refer to steps 2 and 3 to paint hat as desired. Let dry.

8 **For necklace and earrings,** sand 1 side of Shrink-It so that markings will adhere. Be sure to thoroughly sand both vertically and horizontally. Using black marker, trace seed package pattern 3 times on sanded side of Shrink-It. (Marker ink may run on sanded surface; runs will shrink and disappear during baking.) Using scalloped-edge scissors, cut out each design, adding ⅛" all around. Use colored pencils to color each design. (Remember that colors will be more intense after shrinking.) Punch hole in center top of 1 design. Place designs on baking board and bake in oven as described on page 143.

9 Apply 1 coat of sealer to each design. Let dry. To assemble necklace, attach jump ring to hole in punched design, using needlenose pliers. Thread jump ring on satin cording. Thread beads on cording as desired, knotting cording to secure beads. Glue 1 bead to each end of cording, using Designer Tacky Glue. Let dry. Sand back of remaining designs. Sand metal disk of each earring back. Glue 1 earring back to back of each design, using Designer Tacky Glue. Let dry.

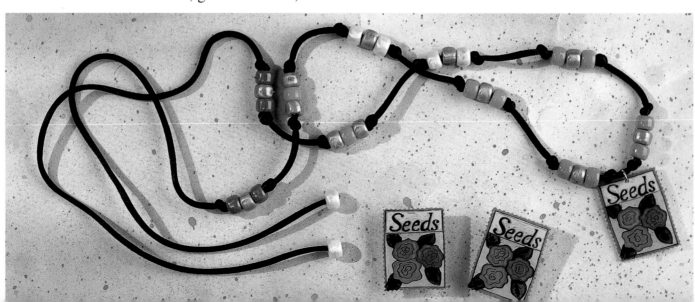

Flowery Shoes & Cap

Use a pencil eraser to paint bright summertime blossoms on a
pair of white sneakers and a plain cap.

Materials (for both)
Pattern on page 62
White canvas shoes
White baseball cap
Fun Foam scrap
6 pencils with erasers
Aleene's Tacky Glue™
Acrylic paints: gold, light blue, pink, medium
    purple, dark purple, green
Waxed paper
2 (28") lengths each ⅛"-wide satin ribbon:
    lavender, purple, magenta, light blue
Assorted wooden beads to coordinate with ribbons

Directions
1 Remove shoelaces; set aside for another use.
Wash shoes and cap; do not use fabric softener.

Let air dry. Stuff wads of clean paper or fabric
inside shoes and cap to provide a firm surface for
painting.

2 Transfer leaf pattern to Fun Foam scrap and
cut out. Glue leaf to eraser of 1 pencil. Let dry.

3 To paint flowers on shoes and cap, pour a
puddle of paint on waxed paper. Dip pencil
eraser into paint and dot on shoe or cap. Use clean
eraser for each color of paint. In same manner, dip
Fun Foam leaf into green paint and press on shoe
or cap. Repeat until desired effect is achieved. Let
dry.

4 For each shoe, handling 1 ribbon of each
color as 1, lace shoe with ribbons. Thread 1
bead on each ribbon end and knot to secure.

5 Do not wash shoes for at least 1 week. Wash
by hand and air dry.

Glittery Fish

Use simple freezer paper stencils to cover a jacket with an undersea scene. Embellish an oversize T-shirt with these fish for a swimsuit cover-up.

Materials

Patterns on page 63
Sweatshirt jacket
Cardboard covered with waxed paper
Freezer paper
Aleene's OK to Wash-It™ Glue
Paintbrush
2 or 3 colors fine glitter for each fish
Dimensional paints: green glitter, gold glitter, assorted colors to match fish
3 to 4 buttons in assorted sizes and colors for bubbles for each fish
Aleene's Jewel-It™ Glue

Directions

1 Wash and dry jacket; do not use fabric softener in washer or dryer. Place cardboard covered with waxed paper inside jacket.

2 For each stencil, cut a piece of freezer paper 1" larger all around than pattern. Centering pattern on freezer paper piece, transfer fish pattern to freezer paper. (You will need a separate piece for each fish to be stenciled on jacket.) Cut out and discard fish. Arrange 1 stencil, wax side down, in desired position on jacket. Press with iron for a few seconds to adhere to jacket. Brush a thin coat of OK to Wash-It Glue on jacket inside stencil. Sprinkle wet glue with 2 or 3 colors of glitter. Let dry. Shake off excess glitter. Remove freezer paper stencil. Repeat to stencil additional fish on jacket.

3 Using dimensional paints, outline each fish, add fins and eyes to each fish, and draw seaweed and fishhook. Let dry.

4 Using Jewel-It Glue, glue 3 or 4 buttons to jacket above each fish for bubbles. Let dry.

5 Do not wash jacket for at least 2 weeks. Turn jacket wrong side out, wash by hand, and hang to dry.

Foil Jewelry

Glue foil to a cardboard shape and imprint a design in the foil while the glue is still wet for charms that look like antique silver. Combine them with turquoise and silver beads from the crafts store for Southwestern-style jewelry.

Materials (for 1 set)
Patterns on page 63
7" x 9" piece thin cardboard
Aluminum foil
Aleene's Designer Tacky Glue™
Toothpick
Tracing paper
Waxed paper
Black acrylic paint
Paintbrush
Aleene's Matte Right-On Finish™
⅛"-diameter hole punch
48" length black satin cording
Assorted turquoise and silver beads
Needlenose pliers
Silver jewelry findings: 4 silver jump rings, 2 clip earring backs, pin back, 2 (⅝"-diameter) black-and-silver plastic disks

Directions

1 Transfer patterns to cardboard and cut 1 necklace circle, 1 pin rectangle, and 6 feathers. Cut 1 piece of foil slightly larger than each cardboard piece.

2 Working with 1 piece at a time, apply a coat of glue to 1 side of each cardboard piece, using fingers or toothpick. With shiny side up and foil edges extending beyond cardboard edges, press matching piece of foil into glue. Smooth foil with fingers. Trim foil edges, leaving about ¼" all around. Fold excess foil to cardboard and glue, clipping curves as needed.

3 While glue is still wet, use toothpick to imprint design in foil. (Do not press too hard or foil may tear.) For feather, imprint parallel lines to simulate texture of real feather. For necklace circle, use the end of a pen to imprint circles. For pin rectangle, transfer pattern to tracing paper.

Lay tracing paper over foil and lightly trace design using toothpick. Remove tracing paper and press toothpick along indented marks to imprint design.

4 Cut 1 piece of foil to fit back of each design piece and glue in place. Let dry.

5 To antique each piece, pour puddle of black paint on piece of waxed paper. Mix a small amount of water with paint. Brush paint on foil design. Immediately wipe off excess paint with paper towel, leaving paint in crevices to highlight imprinted design. Let dry. Apply a coat of finish to each piece and let dry. Punch holes in each design as indicated on pattern.

6 To assemble necklace, fold satin cording in half. Thread fold through center hole in circle from back to front. Thread ends of cording through fold and pull tight to secure. Thread both pieces of cording through several beads. Knot cording above last bead. Separate cording strands and add beads as desired, knotting cording to secure beads. Knot cording ends. Using needlenose pliers, attach 1 jump ring to 1 feather. Attach feather to punched hole in circle.

7 For each earring, glue 1 turquoise bead to 1 plastic disk. With tip of feather sandwiched between, glue plastic disk and earring back together. Let dry.

8 For pin, glue beads to pin rectangle as desired. Using needlenose pliers, attach 1 jump ring to each remaining feather. Attach feathers to holes in pin rectangle. Center and glue bar pin on back of rectangle.

Sponge-Painted Stars

Shimmery metallic paints turn an inexpensive knit dress into attire fit for a night on the town. Stars cut from pop-up craft sponges make this ensemble so easy, you'll be ready to go in no time.

Materials (for 1 outfit)
Patterns on page 64
Black knit dress
Cardboard covered with waxed paper
Masking tape
Pop-up craft sponges
Waxed paper
Metallic acrylic paints: gold, silver, bronze
Hair dryer (optional)
Dimensional paints: gold, silver, bronze
Black elastic fabric belt

Directions

1 Wash and dry dress; do not use fabric softener in washer or dryer. Place cardboard covered with waxed paper inside dress. Referring to photo for positioning, place a piece of masking tape around dress front from shoulder to shoulder, about 4½" from neckline.

2 Cut 1 (3" x 5") piece of sponge. Place sponge in water to expand, wringing out excess water. Pour a small puddle of gold paint on waxed paper. Dip sponge into paint and blot excess paint on paper towel. Gently press sponge on dress above tape to paint background. Let dry. (If desired, use hair dryer to speed drying time.)

3 Transfer patterns to sponge and cut 1 large star and 1 medium star. Place each sponge in water to expand, wringing out excess water. Pour a small puddle of paint on waxed paper. Dip 1 sponge into paint and blot excess paint on paper towel. Gently press sponge on dress in desired position (see photo). Repeat as desired. Wash sponge thoroughly before dipping into different paint color. Let paint dry. Remove masking tape. Add dots and squiggles with dimensional paints as desired. Let dry.

4 In same manner, paint a 5"-wide band around bottom of dress. Let dry. For belt, transfer pattern to sponge and cut 1 small star. Expand sponge and paint belt as described in steps 2 and 3, using small and medium stars. Let dry.

5 Do not wash dress for at least 1 week. Turn dress wrong side out, wash by hand, and hang to dry.

Bright Hearts & Stars Casual Attire

For lounging around the house, nothing feels better than a sweat suit. But if you sponge-paint your outfit with pink hearts and purple stars, you can wear it to run errands. A jaunty visor completes this sporty set.

Materials (for 1 outfit)
Patterns on page 64
White sweatshirt and sweatpants
Cardboard covered with waxed paper
Masking tape
Pop-up craft sponges
Waxed paper
Acrylic paints: pearlescent lavender, pearlescent pink, dark pink, purple
Hair dryer (optional)
Dimensional paints: pink, purple
White plastic visor
Clear spray sealer

Directions

1 Wash and dry shirt and pants; do not use fabric softener in washer or dryer. Place cardboard covered with waxed paper inside shirt. Referring to photo for positioning, place pieces of masking tape on shirt front from shoulder to shoulder, about 3½" from neckline. Place additional pieces of masking tape across shirt front, spaced approximately 4¾" apart, to create 4 horizontal bands across shirt.

2 Cut 1 (3" x 5") piece of sponge. Place sponge in water to expand, wringing out excess water. Pour a small puddle of pearlescent lavender paint on waxed paper. Dip sponge into paint and blot excess paint on paper towel. Gently press sponge on shirt above first piece of tape to paint background of first band with lavender paint. Repeat to paint background of third and fifth bands with lavender paint. Wash sponge thoroughly. In same manner, paint background of second and fourth bands and sleeves with pearlescent pink paint. Let dry. (If desired, use hair dryer to speed drying time.)

3 Transfer patterns to sponge and cut 1 large star, 1 medium star, 1 large heart, and 1 small heart. Place each sponge in water to expand, wringing out excess water. Pour a small puddle of paint on waxed paper. Dip 1 sponge into paint and blot excess paint on paper towel. Gently press sponge on shirt in desired position (see photo). Repeat as desired. Wash sponge thoroughly before dipping into different paint color. Let paint dry. Remove masking tape. Add dots and squiggles with dimensional paints as desired. Let dry.

4 In same manner, paint pants and visor as desired, omitting background paint. Let dry. Apply 1 coat of spray sealer to visor and let dry.

5 Do not wash shirt and pants for at least 1 week. Turn shirt and pants wrong side out, wash by hand, and hang to dry.

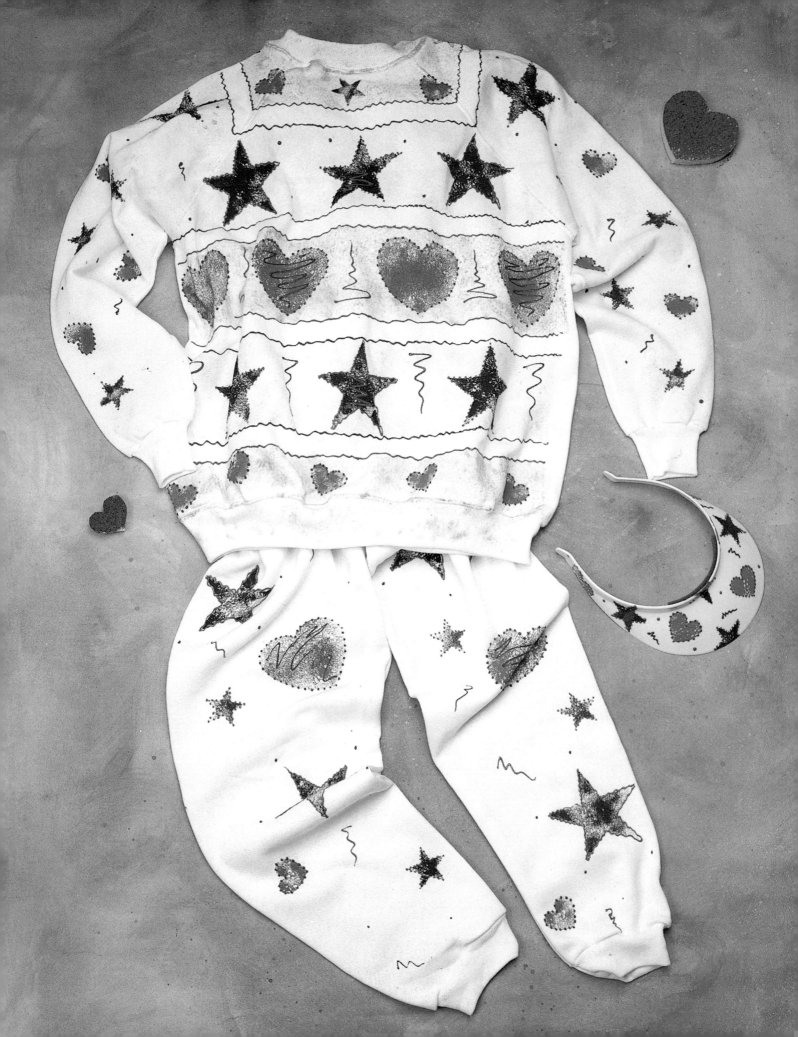

Fused Fleece Pullover

To make a pullover with lapels, cut open a sweatshirt and fold back the cut edges. Fuse fabric to the lapels to add color. Try this with a red or green sweatshirt and holiday fabric, and you'll greet the Christmas season in style.

Materials
Sweatshirt
Cardboard covered with waxed paper
Aleene's Stop Fraying Glue™
Aleene's Fusible Web™
12" x 16" piece print fabric
Aleene's OK to Wash-It™ Glue
2 (28") lengths 1"-wide white eyelet trim
Braided trim to match fabric: 18" length, 28" length
Aleene's Jewel-It™ Glue
12" length ¼"-wide satin ribbon to match braided trim

Directions
Note: See page 136 for tips on working with fusible web.

1 Wash and dry shirt; do not use fabric softener in washer or dryer.

2 To find center front of shirt, fold shirt in half lengthwise, aligning shoulders and side seams. Press along fold. Unfold shirt. Place cardboard covered with waxed paper inside shirt. Beginning at neckline, apply a 17"-long line of Stop Fraying Glue on right side of shirt front along fold line. Let dry. Beginning at neckline and ending ½" before end of glue line, cut shirt open along glue line.

3 To make lapels, fold 1 edge of shirt front over 2¼" at neck, tapering to point at bottom of V opening; press. Unfold lapel and place fusible web on wrong side of lapel. Trace lapel onto paper side of web and cut out pattern. With straight edge aligned with fold line, position web on shirt front and fuse in place. Remove paper and set aside to make print fabric lapels. Refold lapel and fuse to shirt front. Repeat for remaining lapel.

4 Iron fusible web to wrong side of print fabric. Using 1 lapel web paper as pattern, trace lapel on paper side of web, flipping pattern along straight edge to allow for fabric to turn to inside of shirt. Cut out and fuse in place on shirt. Repeat to fuse fabric to other lapel.

5 Referring to *Sweatshirt Diagram* and using OK to Wash-It Glue, glue 1 length of eyelet trim to shirt front along edge of each lapel to waist, leaving ¼" free at each end. Turn trim end at top of lapel to inside of shirt and glue. Turn trim end at waist under ¼" and glue. Let dry.

6 Covering bound edge of eyelet trim and beginning at bottom of V opening in shirt, use Jewel-It Glue to glue 18" braided trim length to shirt front around 1 lapel, leaving ¼" free at end. Covering bound edge of eyelet trim and beginning at top edge of waist ribbing, use Jewel-It Glue to glue remaining length of braided trim to shirt front around other lapel, leaving ¼" free at each end. Turn trim ends at top of each lapel to inside of shirt and glue. Turn trim end at waist under ¼" and glue. Pin trim in place until glue is dry.

7 Tie ribbon in a bow and glue to shirt front at bottom of V opening, using Jewel-It Glue. Let dry.

Sweatshirt Diagram

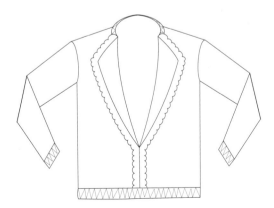

Embossed Glue Barrettes

Draw a design with glue and let the glue dry to create interesting textured surfaces. For an antique effect, lightly apply gold paste paint over black acrylic paint.

Materials (for all items shown)

Patterns on page 65
1 (4") square lightweight cardboard for each barrette
2 plastic headbands
Fine-grade sandpaper
Aleene's Tacky Glue™
Aleene's Fine-Line Syringe™ Glue Applicator
Black acrylic paint
Paintbrush
Gold paste paint
2 French-clasp barrettes
Rubber bands

Directions

Note: See page 65 for directions on making a tape tip for glue bottle instead of using syringe.

1 For hearts barrette, transfer pattern to cardboard and cut 3 hearts. For geometric barrette, transfer pattern to cardboard and cut 1. For headbands, lightly sand each plastic headband to roughen surface so that glue will adhere.

2 Referring to patterns and photo and using syringe, apply glue to 1 side of each cardboard piece and headband to create embossed glue design. Let dry.

3 Paint front of each piece black. Let dry. To add gold highlights to each piece, rub finger in gold paste paint, wipe off excess on paper towel, and gently rub finger over embossed glue design. Continue adding gold to each piece until desired effect is achieved. Let dry.

4 For hearts barrette, overlap hearts slightly and glue together. Let dry. For each barrette, center and glue 1 French-clasp barrette on back of each embossed glue design. Use rubber bands to hold each barrette together until glue is dry.

Evening Bag & Shoe Clips

Create quick evening wear accessories with scraps of elegant fabric and a few trims.

Materials (for both)
7½" x 25" piece black crushed velvet
Aleene's OK to Wash-It™ Glue
60" length black-and-silver cording
Aleene's Jewel-It™ Glue
1 (⅝") black button
Black thread and needle
2 (10") lengths ⅛"-wide black satin ribbon
2 (3") lengths 26-gauge florist's wire
2 silver metallic ribbon roses
2 shoe clips
1 pair black evening shoes

Directions

1 Referring to *Evening Bag Diagram,* cut purse from velvet. Cut 2 (3½"-diameter) circles from remaining velvet for shoe clips; set aside. Turn under ½" around edges of purse. Using OK to Wash-It Glue, glue hems in following order: bottom, sides, and then top. Pin hems in place until glue is dry. With wrong sides facing, fold fabric along fold line 1 and glue sides together, using OK to Wash-It Glue. Pin sides together until glue is dry.

2 With cording ends butted together, glue cording to inside flap of purse along fold line 2, using Jewel-It Glue. Let dry. Glue button to right side of flap, using Jewel-It Glue. Let dry.

3 For each shoe clip, run a gathering thread around edge of 1 fabric circle, about ¼" from edge. Pull tightly to gather circle into a fabric yo-yo. Using florist's wire to secure bow, make a multilooped bow with 1 length of ribbon. With yo-yo gathered side down and using Jewel-It Glue, center and glue multilooped bow to fabric yo-yo. Glue 1 ribbon rose on top of bow. Let dry. Stitch 1 shoe clip to back of yo-yo. Put 1 shoe clip on each shoe.

Evening Bag Diagram
All hems are ½".

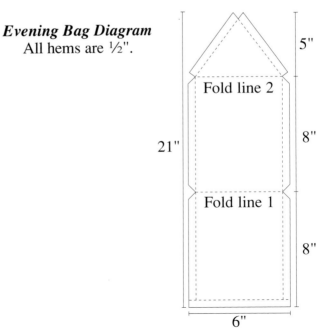

Window Screen Jewelry
Directions are on page 45.

Small
Star

Large
Star

Gardener's Delight
Directions are on pages 47 and 48.

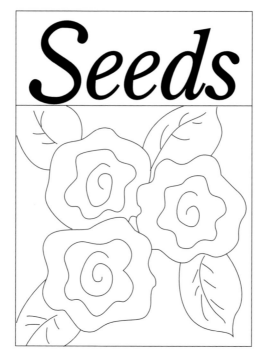

Seed Package

Flowery Shoes & Cap
Directions are on page 49.

Leaf

Glittery Fish

Directions are on page 51.

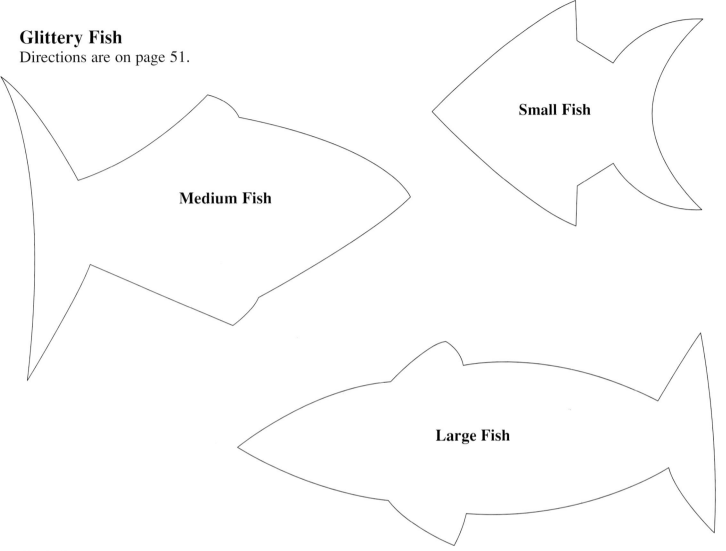

Small Fish

Medium Fish

Large Fish

Foil Jewelry

Directions are on page 53.

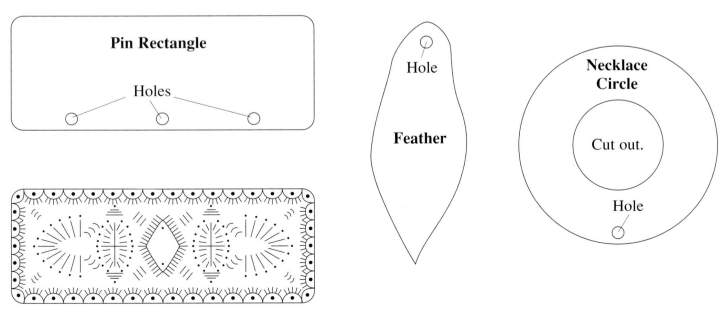

Pin Rectangle

Holes

Hole

Feather

Necklace Circle

Cut out.

Hole

Pin Design

Sponge-Painted Stars
Directions are on page 54.

Bright Hearts & Stars Casual Attire
Directions are on page 56.

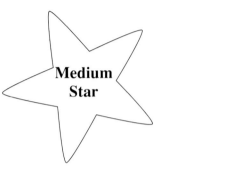

Bright Hearts & Stars Casual Attire
Directions are on page 56.

Embossed Glue Barrettes

Directions are on page 60.

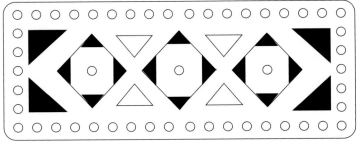

Geometric Barrette Design and Pattern

Heart

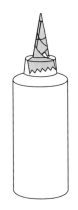

Flower Headband Design

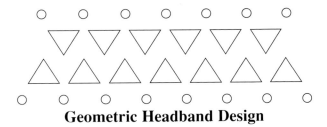

Geometric Headband Design

Tape Tip Diagram

Refer to directions for Embossed Glue Barrettes on page 60.

 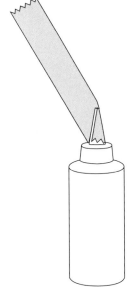 

1. Using 4"-long piece of transparent tape, align 1 long edge of tape with edge of nozzle as shown. Press tape firmly to nozzle to prevent leaks.

2. Rotate bottle to wrap tape around tip.

3. Continue rotating bottle and wrapping tape until tape reverses direction and winds back down toward bottle.

4. Press tail of tape to bottle for easy removal.

Crafts for Kids

Crafting with your children can be rewarding for you as well as for them. In this chapter, you'll find lots of ways to share your love of crafts with your youngsters.

Pom-pom Critter Magnets

Glue pom-poms together to make this trio of refrigerator magnets. Even young children can assemble these critters, especially if you precut the pieces for them.

Materials (for 3 critters)

For each: Aleene's Tacky Glue™
½"-diameter magnet

For cat with tiny mice: Patterns on page 90
Pom-poms: 1 (2"-diameter) white, 1 (1½"-diameter) white, 2 (¼"-diameter) white, 6 (¼"-diameter) gray
Felt scraps: white, dark gray
2 (4-mm) black beads
Fine-tip permanent black marker
7" length ¼"-wide light blue satin ribbon
Light gray paper scraps
⅛"-diameter hole punch
Light gray embroidery floss

For mouse: Patterns on page 90
Gray pom-poms: 1 (2"-diameter), 1 (1½"-diameter), 2 (¼"-diameter)
Dark gray felt scraps
Pop-up craft sponge scrap
2 (4-mm) black beads

For bunny: Patterns on page 90
Pom-poms: 1 (2"-diameter) white, 1 (1½"-diameter) white, 2 (½"-diameter) pink
Felt scraps: white, dark gray, orange, green
White paper scrap
2 (¼"-diameter) black half-round bead eyes
Fine-tip permanent black marker
Toothpick
Green colored pencil

Directions

1 **For each,** glue 2"-diameter pom-pom for body to 1½"-diameter pom-pom for head to form critter. Glue magnet to 1½"-diameter pom-pom. Let dry.

2 **For cat with tiny mice,** transfer patterns and cut 2 cat ears and 2 arms from white felt and 1 cat nose from dark gray felt. Referring to photo, glue ears and arms in place on pom-pom critter; glue ¼"-diameter white pom-poms side by side on head to form cheeks. Let dry. Glue nose to cheeks. Glue beads in place for eyes. Let dry. Using black marker, write "Friends Forever" on ribbon at 1 end. Wrap and glue ribbon in place around cat's neck. Let dry.

3 For each tiny mouse, glue 2 (¼"-diameter) gray pom-poms together. Let dry. Punch 2 circles from light gray paper. Glue paper circles in place on pom-pom mouse for ears. Using black marker, make 3 dots on mouse head for eyes and mouth. Cut 1 (1¾") length of 6-strand embroidery floss for tail. Knot 1 end of floss. Glue other end of floss to pom-pom mouse. Let dry. Referring to photo, glue mice in place on cat. Let dry.

4 **For mouse,** transfer patterns and cut 2 mouse ears, 2 arms, and 1 mouse nose from dark gray felt and 1 cheese from pop-up craft sponge. Referring to photo, glue ears and arms in place on pom-pom critter; glue ¼"-diameter gray pom-poms side by side on head to form cheeks. Let dry. Glue nose to cheeks. Glue beads in place for eyes. Let dry.

5 Dip cheese sponge piece in water to expand. Wring out water and let sponge dry. Referring to photo, glue sponge to mouse. Let dry.

6 **For bunny,** transfer patterns and cut 2 bunny ears and 2 arms from white felt, 1 bunny nose from dark gray felt, 1 carrot from orange felt, 1 carrot top from green felt, and 1 teeth from white paper. From remaining white paper, cut 1 (1" x 1¾") piece for sign. Referring to photo, glue ears and arms in place on pom-pom critter; glue ½"-diameter pink pom-poms side by side on head to form cheeks. Let dry. Glue teeth to bunny below cheeks. Glue nose to cheeks. Glue bead eyes in place. Let dry.

7 Using black marker, draw detail lines on carrot (see photo). Glue carrot top to carrot. Let dry. Apply glue to 1 (1") end of paper sign. Press toothpick into glue and wrap paper around toothpick once. Let dry. Using green pencil, write "Eat Your Veggies" on sign. Glue carrot and sign to bunny. Let dry.

Heidi's Hint

To glue pom-poms, separate the pom-pom fuzz with your fingers and then squeeze in the glue. If you apply the glue inside the fuzz instead of on the fuzz ends, your project will stay together more securely.

Kite Appliqué Outfit

Bright fabric scraps decorate a T-shirt and denim jeans with high-flying fun. Fusing appliqués to clothing is a great way to freshen up a hand-me-down or a not yet worn-out pair of pants.

Materials (for 1 outfit)
Patterns on page 90
White T-shirt
Denim jeans
Fabric scraps: green, blue, hot pink, purple, dark pink
Aleene's Fusible Web™
Cardboard covered with waxed paper
Dimensional paints: blue, green, pink, purple, gold, gray

Directions
Note: See page 136 for tips on working with fusible web.

1 Wash and dry shirt, jeans, and fabric scraps; do not use fabric softener in washer or dryer. Iron fusible web to wrong side of fabric scraps.

2 Transfer patterns to paper side of web and cut 1 kite each from green, blue, hot pink, and purple; cut 23 bows as desired from fabric scraps. Referring to photo, fuse kites and bows to shirt and jeans. For shirt and jeans, place cardboard covered with waxed paper inside garment. Embellish fused appliqués with dimensional paints as desired (see photo). Paint kite string with gray dimensional paint. Let dry.

3 Do not wash garments for at least 1 week. Turn garments wrong side out, wash by hand, and hang to dry.

Fancy Footwear

Pair dressed-up sneakers with decorated socks or tights for accessories to outfit your little darling for any occasion.

Materials (for all items shown)

For each: 1 pair white sneakers

For lacy set: 1 pair lace-trimmed ecru socks
Craft knife
Clothespins
1 length 1"-wide ecru lace trim to fit around
    each shoe
Aleene's OK to Wash-It™ Glue
2 (4"-diameter) ecru doilies
Ecru thread and needle
Assorted buttons and pearls
4 ecru ribbon roses with leaves
Aleene's Jewel-It™ Glue
Cardboard scrap covered with waxed paper

For starry set: Pattern on page 90
1 pair white tights
Fun Foam scraps
6 pencils with erasers
Aleene's Designer Tacky Glue™
Acrylic paints: green, teal, yellow, pink,
    purple, red
Waxed paper
14 plastic star-shaped beads in assorted colors
Empty plastic bottle

For personalized set: Alphabet on page 91
1 pair socks
Aleene's Opake Shrink-It™ Plastic
Fine-grade sandpaper
Fine-tip permanent black marker
Colored pencils
1/8"-diameter hole punch
Aleene's Baking Board or nonstick cookie sheet
Thread and needle

Directions

1 **For lacy set or starry set,** remove shoelaces from shoes. Wash shoes and socks or tights; do not use fabric softener in washer. Let shoes air dry. Dry socks or tights; do not use fabric softener in dryer.

2 **For lacy set,** push tongue of 1 shoe completely inside shoe toward toe area. Using craft knife, make a 1/2"-long slit along seam on each side of shoe beside eye closest to toe. Turn down each eye edge of shoe and hold in place with clothespins. Pull tongue out of shoe and fold down over toe area of shoe. Hold tongue in place with clothespin. Beginning at 1 edge of tongue, glue 1 lace length around shoe, using OK to Wash-It Glue and following contour of eyelet flap. Let dry. Glue eyelet flaps and tongue to outside of shoe, using OK to Wash-It Glue. Use clothespins to hold glued areas together until glue is dry. Repeat for second shoe.

3 To decorate each shoe, run a gathering thread around 1 doily, 2" from edge. Pull to gather and secure thread. Glue 1 doily to shoe over tongue, using OK to Wash-It Glue. Pin doily in place until glue is dry. Referring to photo and using Jewel-It Glue, attach buttons, pearls, and 1 ribbon rose to shoe. Let dry. To decorate each sock, place cardboard scrap covered with waxed paper inside cuff area of sock. Glue buttons, pearls, and 1 ribbon rose to cuff of sock. Let dry.

4 **For starry set,** stuff wads of clean paper or fabric inside shoes to provide a firm surface for decorating. Transfer star pattern to Fun Foam and cut out. Glue star to pencil eraser. Repeat to make 1 star stamp for each paint color. Let dry.

5 To paint stars on shoes, pour puddle of paint on waxed paper. Dip Fun Foam star into paint and press on shoes. Repeat until desired effect is achieved, using separate stamp for each paint color. Let dry. Referring to photo, put laces in shoes, threading star beads on laces as desired. To paint stars on tights, place plastic bottle inside 1 leg at a time to provide a firm surface for decorating. In same manner as for shoes, dip star stamps into paint and press on tights until desired effect is achieved. Let dry.

continued on page 74

6 **For personalized set,** sand 1 side of Shrink-It so that markings will adhere. Be sure to thoroughly sand both vertically and horizontally. Using black marker, trace desired name or monogram for each shoe nameplate and desired name or monogram for each sock on sanded side of Shrink-It. (Marker ink may run on sanded surface; runs will shrink and disappear during baking.) Use colored pencils to color each design. (Remember that colors will be more intense after shrinking.)

7 For nameplate, cut out a rectangle larger than name or monogram, leaving space at each end for slits for laces. Cut a ¼" x ½" slit in each end of nameplate. For sock decoration, cut out each letter. Punch holes in each letter as indicated on pattern. Place designs on baking board and bake in oven as described on page 143.

8 Referring to photo, thread 1 nameplate on each shoelace and put laces in shoes. Stitch letters to each sock cuff as desired.

9 Do not wash shoes and socks or tights for at least 1 week. For shoes, wash by hand and let air dry. For socks or tights, turn wrong side out, wash by hand, and hang to dry.

A Boy's Bulletin Board

Keep notes and schedules handy with a bulletin board featuring a felt dinosaur.

Materials
Alphabet on page 91
Patterns on page 92
Cork bulletin board with wooden frame
Blue acrylic paint
Paintbrush
Felt: rust, dark brown, green, scraps in assorted colors
Aleene's Fusible Web™
Aleene's Tacky Glue™
¼"-diameter black half-round bead eye

Directions
Note: See page 136 for tips on working with fusible web.

1 Paint bulletin board frame blue. Let dry. Iron fusible web to felt. (Pieces will not be fused to bulletin board. Applying web adds stability to felt and makes it easier to cut out pieces.) Transfer patterns to paper side of web and cut 1 rust dinosaur, 1 rust eyelid, 2 rust legs, and 14 green leaves. For tree trunk, cut 1 (1¼" x 16") strip from dark brown, tapering 1 end of strip to a point. Reverse patterns for letters of child's name so that they will be right side up when applied to bulletin board. Transfer letters to paper side of web on assorted felt scraps and cut out. Remove paper backing from web.

2 Referring to photo, glue bead eye, eyelid, and legs to dinosaur. Glue felt pieces to bulletin board. Wrap 1 leaf and tail of dinosaur around edge of board, leaving room to hold pencil (see photo). Let dry.

A Girl's Bulletin Board

Lace and hearts frame a bulletin board that's perfect for a little girl's room.

Materials
Alphabet on page 91
Patterns on page 93
Cork bulletin board with wooden frame
Pink acrylic paint
Paintbrush
Aleene's Designer Tacky Glue™
1¾"-wide white lace trim to fit around bulletin board
Fabric scraps: assorted pink prints, dark pink
Aleene's Fusible Web™
Lightweight cardboard

Directions
Note: See page 136 for tips on working with fusible web.

1 Paint bulletin board frame pink. Let dry. Glue lace trim to back of bulletin board so that lace extends beyond edge of bulletin board. Let dry.

2 For pencil pocket, cut 1 (3¼" x 3½") piece from 1 pink print. Turn under ½" along each 3½" edge and glue. Let dry for a few minutes. Turn under ¾" along each 3¼" edge and glue. Let dry. With side edges about 1¾" apart, glue side and bottom edges of pocket in place at bottom left corner of bulletin board. Use pins to hold pocket in place until glue is dry.

3 Iron fusible web to wrong side of remaining fabric scraps. For each heart, cut 1 piece each of fabric and cardboard slightly larger than pattern. Transfer heart pattern to cardboard. Fuse fabric to unmarked side of cardboard. Cut out heart. Repeat to make 1 heart A, 2 heart Bs, 2 heart Cs, 3 heart Ds, and 2 heart Es. Glue 1 heart D to pencil pocket. Referring to photo for positioning, glue remaining hearts to bulletin board. Let dry. Reverse patterns for letters of child's name so that they will be right side up when applied to bulletin board. Transfer letters to paper side of web on dark pink fabric. Cut out letters and fuse to hearts (see photo).

Barrette & Earring Holder

Barrettes and earrings stay organized and easy to find
with this braided fabric holder.

Materials

Patterns on page 93
Fabric: 3 (2¾" x 36") strips assorted pink prints,
    5½" square pink print
3 (1" x 36") strips batting
Aleene's Fusible Web™
Aleene's Designer Tacky Glue™
5½" square lightweight cardboard
2 (14") lengths 1"-wide white eyelet trim
5½" square pink plastic canvas
1 yard ⅛"-wide pink satin ribbon
Tiny dried flowers
Pink silk rosebud
10" length ⅜"-wide pink satin ribbon

Directions

Note: See page 136 for tips on working with
fusible web.

1 Lay 1 fabric strip right side down on work
surface. With ends aligned, place 1 batting
strip in center of fabric strip. Fold over both long
edges of fabric strip to form a 1¼"-wide strip and
press. Cut 1 (½" x 36") strip of fusible web.
Remove paper from web. Place web between over-
lapped edges of fabric strip and fuse. Repeat with
remaining fabric and batting strips. Stack strips on
top of each other with seam sides down and glue
together 1½" at 1 end. Let dry. Braid strips loosely
and glue at end to secure. Let dry.

2 Transfer pattern for heart A to cardboard and
cut out. Transfer pattern for heart A to pink
print fabric square and cut out, adding ½" all
around. Center and glue cardboard heart on wrong
side of fabric heart. Squeeze a line of glue around
edge of cardboard heart. Fold excess fabric to cardboard, clipping curves as needed, and press into
glue. Glue 1 length of eyelet trim to back of heart
so that eyelet extends beyond edge of heart. Let dry.

3 Transfer pattern for heart A to plastic canvas
and cut out. Glue remaining length of eyelet
trim around edge of plastic canvas heart. Let dry.
Cut 1 (8") length of ⅛"-wide ribbon. Tie ribbon

length in a bow. Glue bow to eyelet trim at top of
plastic canvas heart. Glue 1 end of braided strips
to top back of plastic canvas heart. Let dry.

4 Make a multilooped bow with remaining
⅛"-wide ribbon. Glue bow to top of fabric-
covered heart. Glue tiny dried flowers and silk
rosebud on top of bow. Let dry. Glue remaining
end of braided strips to back of fabric-covered
heart. Fold ⅜"-wide ribbon in half to form a loop.
Glue ribbon ends to back of fabric-covered heart at
top. Let dry.

Noah's Ark Shirt & Necklace

Pairs of Shrink-It animals embellish a fused fabric ark to decorate a T-shirt. Make additional animals as charms for a gold necklace.

Materials (for both)

For each: Patterns on pages 93 and 94
Aleene's Opake Shrink-It™ Plastic
Fine-grade sandpaper
Fine-tip permanent black marker
Colored pencils
Aleene's Baking Board or nonstick cookie sheet
For shirt: White T-shirt
Assorted brown print fabric scraps
Aleene's Fusible Web™
Alphabet on page 91
⅛"-diameter hole punch
Thread in assorted colors and needle
For necklace: ³⁄₁₆"-diameter hole punch
Needlenose pliers
9 gold jump rings
18"-long gold necklace with clasp

Directions

1 **For each animal,** sand 1 side of Shrink-It so that markings will adhere. Be sure to thoroughly sand horizontally and vertically. Using black marker, trace pattern on sanded side of Shrink-It. (Marker ink may run on sanded surface; runs will shrink and disappear during baking.) Refer to photo when drawing partial animals to go on shirt with ark. Use colored pencils to color each design. (Remember that colors will be more intense after shrinking.) Punch hole in design as specified in Step 2 or 4. Place design on baking board and bake in oven as described on page 143.

2 **For shirt,** wash and dry shirt and fabric scraps; do not use fabric softener in washer or dryer. (*Note:* See page 136 for tips on working with fusible web.) Iron fusible web to wrong side of brown print fabrics. Referring to photo, transfer patterns for ark pieces to paper side of web and cut out. Fuse ark pieces to shirt.

3 Referring to Step 1, make Shrink-It decorations for the words "two by two," 1 whole kangaroo, 1 partial kangaroo, 2 seals, 1 monkey, and 2 partial zebras. (*Note:* Reverse patterns as needed to create pairs of animals.) Using ⅛" hole punch, punch 2 holes side by side in each design (except monkey). Punch hole in monkey's hand as indicated on pattern. Shrink designs as described in Step 1. Sew decorations on shirt with matching thread.

4 Do not wash shirt for at least 1 week. Turn shirt wrong side out, wash by hand, and hang to dry.

5 **For necklace,** refer to Step 1 to make 2 elephants, 2 giraffes, 1 lioness, 1 lion, 1 ewe, 1 ram, and 1 monkey for necklace charms. (*Note:* Reverse patterns as needed to create pairs of animals.) Using ³⁄₁₆" hole punch, punch 1 hole in each design to attach charm to necklace. Shrink designs as described in Step 1. Using needlenose pliers, attach 1 jump ring to each charm. Attach jump rings to necklace.

Storage Boxes

Don't throw those boxes away. Cover them with fabric and let your little ones add personal touches. Putting things away will be easy with a set of special boxes.

Materials (for 1 box)
Alphabet on page 91
Patterns on page 95
Cardboard shoe box or gift box
Fabric to cover box
Aleene's Designer Tacky Glue™
Aleene's Fusible Web™
Fabric scraps for appliquéd decorations
Pop-up craft sponge
Acrylic paints in desired colors
Waxed paper
Pencil with eraser

Directions
Note: See page 136 for tips on working with fusible web.

1 To cover shoe box and lid with fabric, measure around sides of box. Measure height of box side. Add ½" all around and cut a strip of fabric to these measurements. Center and glue fabric strip around sides of box, turning raw edges under at ends. Fold excess fabric over top and bottom edges of box and glue. Let dry. Measure width, length, and depth of box lid. Add ½" all around and cut a piece of fabric to these measurements. Lay box lid right side down on wrong side of fabric. Fold and glue edges of fabric to inside of box lid. Let dry. Refer to steps 3 and 4 to decorate box and lid with fabric appliqués or sponge-painted designs.

2 To cover gift box lid with fabric, carefully open lid of box until it lies completely flat. Iron fusible web to wrong side of fabric. Place flattened box lid right side down on paper side of web and trace. Cut out shape, leaving ½" all around. Center and fuse fabric on right side of box lid. Turn under ½" all around and fuse. Refold box lid into its original shape and glue flaps in place. Let dry. Refer to steps 3 and 4 to decorate box lid with fabric appliqués or sponge-painted designs.

3 To decorate box with fabric appliqués, iron fusible web to wrong side of fabric scraps. Transfer desired patterns to paper side of web and cut out. Reverse patterns for letters so that they will be right side up when fused to box. Fuse cutouts to box as desired.

4 To sponge-paint box, transfer swirl pattern to pop-up craft sponge and cut out. Place sponge in water to expand, wringing out excess water. Pour a small puddle of paint on waxed paper. Dip sponge into paint and blot excess paint on paper towel. Gently press sponge on box in desired position. Repeat as desired. Wash sponge thoroughly before dipping into different paint color. Let paint dry. To paint dots on box, dip pencil eraser into paint and dot on box as desired. (Use clean eraser for each color of paint.) Let dry.

ART WORK

PHOTOS

MY STUFF

Animal Cap & Visors

Dress up a few visors and a cap to keep on hand for sunny outings. For a fantastic party game, provide guests with felt and trims and let them decorate their own cap or visor.

Materials (for 1 hat and 2 visors)
For each: Eyelid pattern on page 95
Aleene's Designer Tacky Glue™
2 (1¼"-diameter) packing foam pieces
Black acrylic paint
Paintbrush
For cat: Patterns on page 95
Felt: white, pink, black
2 (2"-diameter) white pom-poms
Brown acrylic paint
6 (2½"-long) pieces black waxed linen thread
Pink baseball cap
16" length ⅜"-wide pink satin ribbon
For cow: Patterns on page 96
Felt: white, pink, black
White plastic visor
Raffia
For frog: Patterns on page 97
Felt: green, red, black
Aleene's Opake Shrink-It™ Plastic scrap
Green plastic visor

Directions

1 **For cat,** transfer patterns to felt and cut 2 white eyelids, 1 white cat head, 2 pink inner ears, and 1 black nose. Glue inner ears in place on head. Glue pom-poms side by side on head to form cheeks. Glue nose to cheeks. Let dry. For eyes, paint rounded side of each foam piece with black for pupil and brown for iris. Let dry. Referring to photo, glue eyes and eyelids to head. Glue 3 lengths of waxed linen thread to each pom-pom cheek for whiskers. Let dry. Glue cat head to front of hat. Tie ribbon in a bow. Glue bow to hat at top of cat head. Let dry.

2 **For cow,** transfer patterns to felt and cut 2 white eyelids, 1 white cow head, 1 white cow muzzle, 2 pink nostrils, 1 pink tongue, 3 black spots for head and muzzle, 1 black whole spot, and 1 black half spot. Glue spots and nostrils in place on head and muzzle. With top edge of muzzle on top, overlap muzzle and head ¼" and glue together. Let dry. For eyes, paint rounded side of each foam piece with black for pupils. Let dry. Referring to photo, glue eyes and eyelids to head. Let dry. Glue cow head to front of visor, gluing ¼" of straight edge of tongue inside mouth (see photo). Glue whole spot and half spot to visor. Glue strands of raffia to tongue. Let dry.

3 **For frog,** transfer patterns and cut 2 green eyelids, 1 green face, 1 red tongue, 1 black bug, and 1 Shrink-It bug wings. For eyes, paint rounded side of each foam piece with black for pupils. Let dry. Referring to photo, glue eyes and eyelids to head. Let dry. Glue frog head to visor, gluing ¼" of straight edge of tongue inside mouth (see photo). Glue bottom of tongue to edge of face about 1½" from pointed end. Let dry. Fold bug wings in half as indicated on pattern. Glue wings to bug. Let dry. Glue bug to tongue. Let dry.

Easy Block Printing

Make your own stamps and use paint or stamp pads to block-print on paper or fabric.

Materials (for making stamp)
Patterns on page 97
Fun Foam
Scalloped-edge scissors (optional)
Foam-core board scrap
Aleene's Designer Tacky Glue™
Acrylic paints or stamp pad
Paintbrush

Directions
Note: Use Fun Foam stamps to embellish all kinds of everyday items. In the photos on these pages, Heidi has used the stamps on small stationery cards, a purchased gift box, a canvas lunch sack, a white T-shirt, and a fabric fanny pack. By printing a design on kraft paper, Heidi creates a unique and inexpensive gift wrap paper.

1 Transfer pattern to Fun Foam and cut out. For fish, cut wavy edge with scalloped-edge scissors. Center and glue foam cutouts on foam-core board scrap, leaving space between pieces as indicated on pattern. Let dry. Trim edges of foam-core to within ¼" of design.

2 Paint foam stamp with desired color of acrylic paint or press foam stamp on stamp pad. Position stamp on printing surface and press firmly, being sure all areas of stamp come into contact with printing surface. Carefully lift stamp off printing surface. (*Hint:* It is a good idea to practice on a piece of paper to determine the correct amount of pressure and paint needed to achieve the desired effect.) Apply a fresh coat of paint to stamp and reapply to printing surface as desired. Let dry. To apply a different paint to stamp, let paint on stamp dry and then apply new color. To use several colors on same stamp, paint each area of foam cutout with desired color.

Print bright suns and colorful rainbows on a T-shirt or a fanny pack. To make a greeting card, fold a piece of paper in half and print the design on the card front. For one of the cards shown in this photo, Heidi used a fine-tip permanent black marker to add an outline of dots to the printed design.

Decorate a gift box or kraft paper with a printed design to add a handmade touch to gift-giving. A matching greeting card or a gift tag is the finishing touch. Apply printed tropical fish to a purchased canvas bag and you'll never again mistake someone else's lunch for your own.

These Fun Foam stamps are easy enough for children to use. Older children can help make the stamps. For the younger set, make the stamps ahead of time and then help them embellish all kinds of items. The stamps are reusable, so keep a wide selection of paint colors on hand to fill rainy days with crafting or to quickly create a last-minute card or gift wrap.

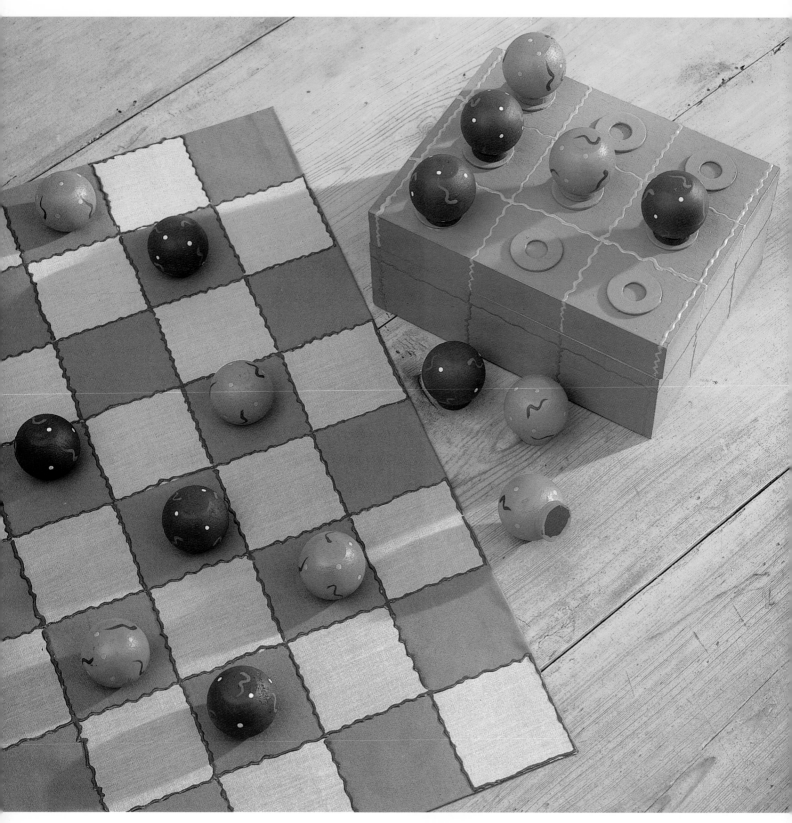

Tic-tac-toe & Checkers Set

With a little paint, wooden balls become game pieces. Let your children select their favorite colors to make this unusual game set with its own storage box.

Materials (for 1 set)

Wooden box
9 (1"-diameter) metal washers
Aleene's Designer Tacky Glue™
24 (1¼"-diameter) wooden balls, each with ½"-diameter hole
8 (¾"-diameter) magnets
Acrylic paints: light purple, pink, dark purple, teal
Paintbrushes: ½" shader, fine-tip
Toothpick
Dimensional paints: teal, pink, purple
1 (17½") square each pink and teal fabric
Aleene's Fusible Web™

Directions

Note: See page 136 for tips on working with fusible web.

1 Lightly draw a 3 x 3 grid on top of box lid. Center and glue 1 washer inside each square of grid. Let dry. Glue 1 magnet each to 8 balls, covering holes. Let dry.

2 Paint entire surface of box light purple. Let dry. Paint 4 balls with magnets and 8 balls without magnets pink. Paint remaining 12 balls dark purple. Let dry. Paint dark purple squiggles on pink balls and pink squiggles on dark purple balls. Let dry. Using toothpick, dot teal paint on pink balls and light purple paint on dark purple balls. Referring to photo and using dimensional paint, draw teal grid on box lid and pink grid on sides of box bottom. Let dry.

3 Wash and dry fabric; do not use fabric softener in washer or dryer. Fuse ½"-wide strips of web to each edge on wrong side of pink fabric. To hem fabric, turn under ½" along each edge and fuse. Iron fusible web to wrong side of teal fabric. Cut 32 (2") squares from teal fabric. Arrange teal squares, web side down, on right side of pink fabric to form checkerboard. Fuse squares in place. Outline teal squares with purple dimensional paint. Let dry.

Dinosaur Jacket

Most little boys are very fond of dinosaurs. Turn a sweatshirt into a nifty jacket embellished with a fused fabric prehistoric creature.

Materials

Patterns on page 92
Blue child-sized sweatshirt
Fabric scraps: light rust minidot, medium rust print, green, brown print
Cardboard covered with waxed paper
Aleene's Stop Fraying Glue™
Aleene's Fusible Web™
Dimensional paints: metallic brown, black, green, brown

Directions

Note: See page 136 for tips on working with fusible web.

1 Wash and dry shirt and fabric scraps; do not use fabric softener in washer or dryer. To find center front of shirt, fold shirt in half lengthwise, aligning shoulders and side seams. Press along fold. Unfold shirt. Place cardboard covered with waxed paper inside shirt. Squeeze a line of glue on right side of shirt front along fold line. Let dry. Cut shirt open along glue line. Turn under ¼" along each cut edge and glue for hem. Pin hem in place until glue is dry.

2 Iron fusible web to wrong side of fabric scraps. Transfer patterns to paper side of web and cut 1 dinosaur from light rust minidot, 2 legs from medium rust print, and 8 leaves from green. For tree trunk, cut 1 (1½" x 10") strip from brown print, tapering 1 end of strip to a point. Referring to photo, fuse appliqués to shirt. (*Hint:* To position dinosaur, place middle of dinosaur's body beneath armhole, with dinosaur head on front of shirt and tail wrapped around to back of shirt.) Embellish fused appliqués and draw leaves with dimensional paint. Let dry.

3 Do not wash jacket for at least 1 week. Turn jacket wrong side out, wash by hand, and hang to dry.

Embellishing with Fabric Motifs

Use Aleene's Ultra-Hold Fusible Web™ to apply motifs cut from novelty print fabric to a purchased nylon backpack like the one shown here. A letters guide (found in most crafts or art supply stores) makes it a snap to add words to the design with shiny dimensional paint. With as little as ¼ yard of fabric, you can turn a plain item into a personalized treasure. (For tips on working with fusible web, see page 136.) Choosing from the wide variety of print fabrics available may be the hardest part of embellishing this backpack. Try this idea on any number of projects. For items that cannot be ironed, use Aleene's Tacky Glue™ or Designer Tacky Glue™ to adhere the fabric cutout to the item. Use the fusible web on the wrong side of the fabric to add stability

to the cutout and to keep the edges from fraying.

Other items you can decorate include: a plastic pencil box, a sleeping bag or a pillowcase, a fabric tote bag for ballet clothes, a camera bag, a laundry bag, an umbrella, and a canvas or nylon lunch sack.

Pom-pom Critter Magnets

Directions are on pages 68 and 69.

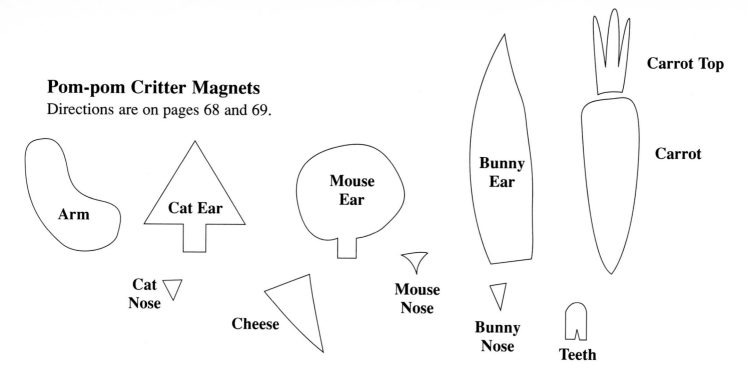

Arm

Cat Ear

Cat Nose

Cheese

Mouse Ear

Mouse Nose

Bunny Ear

Bunny Nose

Teeth

Carrot Top

Carrot

Kite Appliqué Outfit

Directions are on page 70.

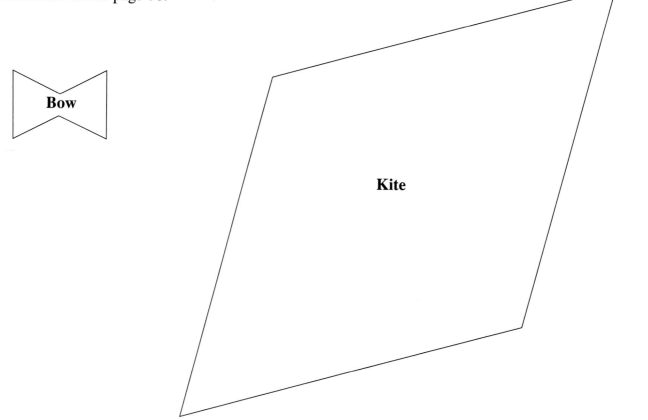

Bow

Kite

Fancy Footwear

Directions are on pages 73 and 74.

Star

Alphabet

Circles on letters indicate placement of holes for
use with Shrink-It designs.

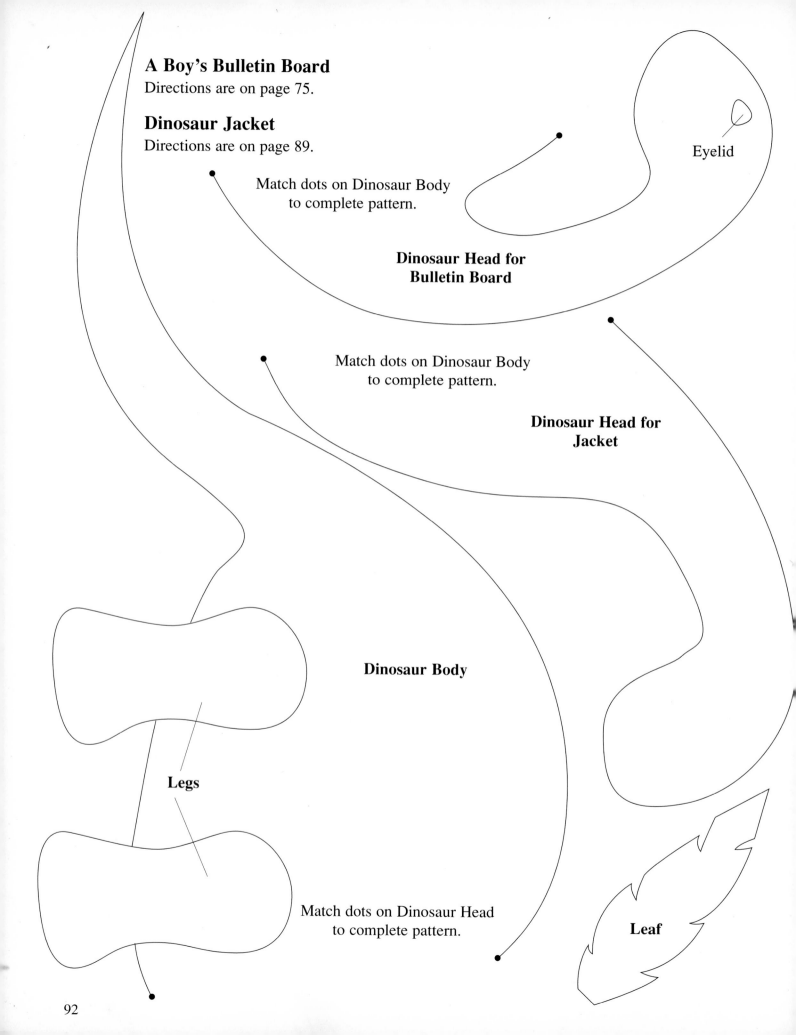

A Boy's Bulletin Board
Directions are on page 75.

Dinosaur Jacket
Directions are on page 89.

Match dots on Dinosaur Body
to complete pattern.

Eyelid

**Dinosaur Head for
Bulletin Board**

Match dots on Dinosaur Body
to complete pattern.

**Dinosaur Head for
Jacket**

Dinosaur Body

Legs

Match dots on Dinosaur Head
to complete pattern.

Leaf

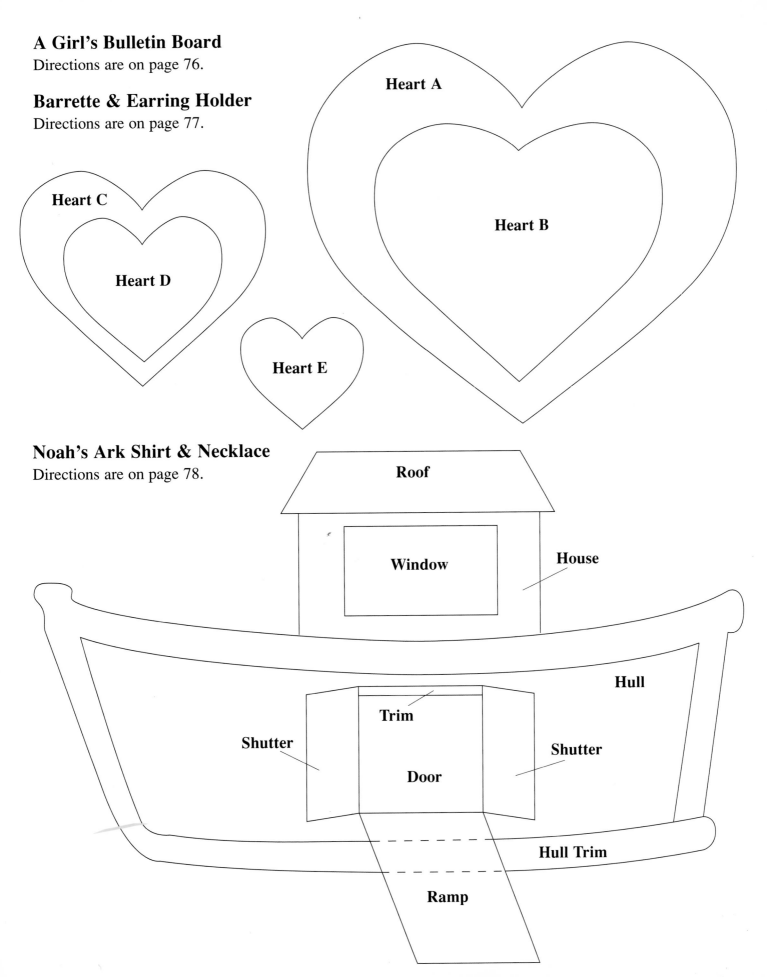

A Girl's Bulletin Board
Directions are on page 76.

Barrette & Earring Holder
Directions are on page 77.

Heart A

Heart C

Heart B

Heart D

Heart E

Noah's Ark Shirt & Necklace
Directions are on page 78.

Roof

Window

House

Hull

Trim

Shutter

Shutter

Door

Hull Trim

Ramp

Noah's Ark Shirt & Necklace
Directions are on page 78.

Lion Head
For lion, use lioness body and substitute lion head.

Lioness

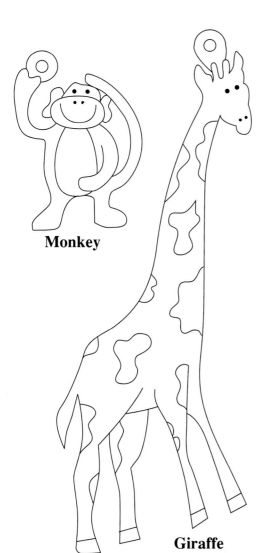

Monkey

Giraffe

Elephant

Kangaroo
For male kangaroo, omit pouch and baby.

Ram

Ewe

Zebra

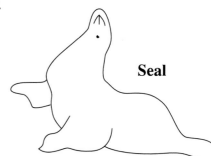

Seal

94

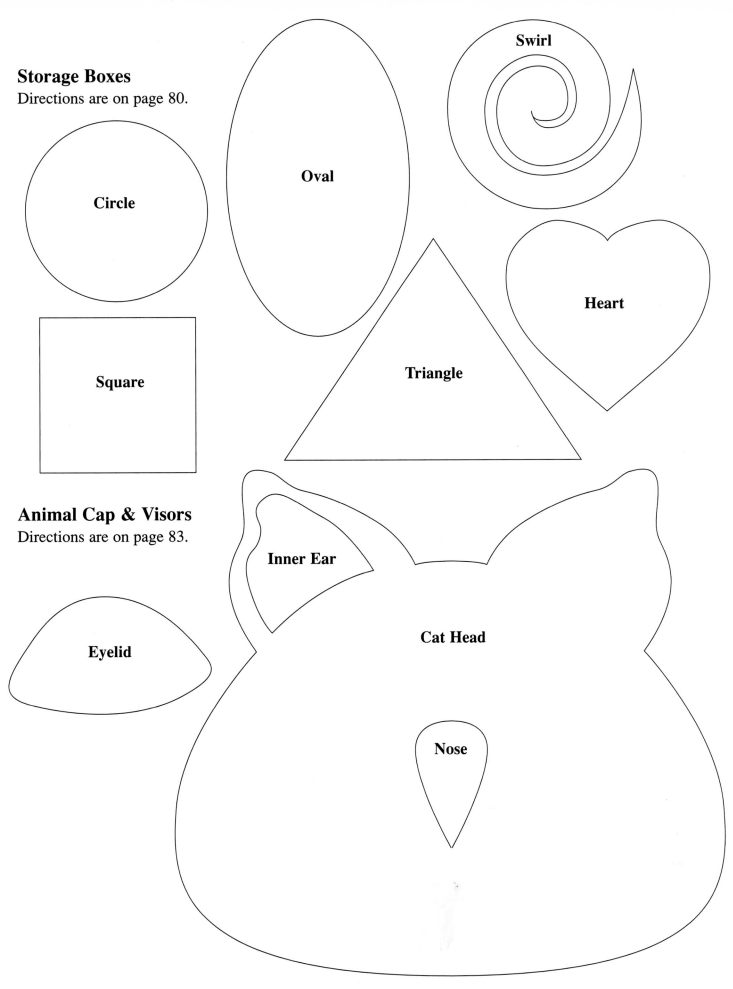

Storage Boxes
Directions are on page 80.

Circle

Oval

Swirl

Square

Triangle

Heart

Animal Cap & Visors
Directions are on page 83.

Inner Ear

Cat Head

Eyelid

Nose

Animal Cap & Visors

Directions are on page 83.

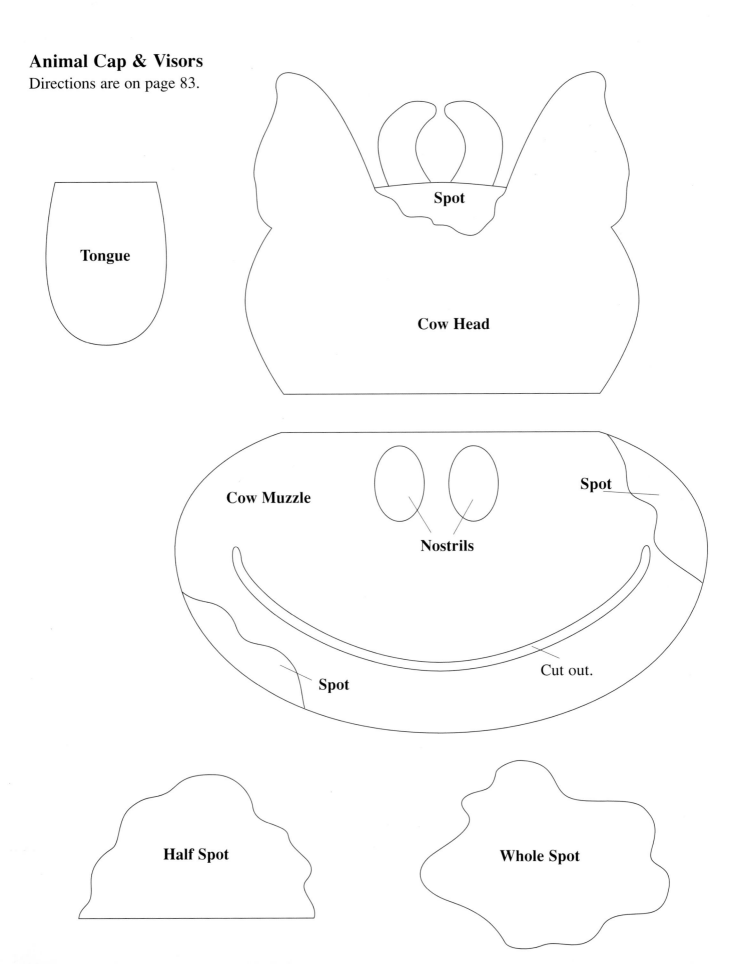

Tongue

Spot

Cow Head

Cow Muzzle

Nostrils

Spot

Spot

Cut out.

Half Spot

Whole Spot

Animal Cap & Visors

Directions are on page 83.

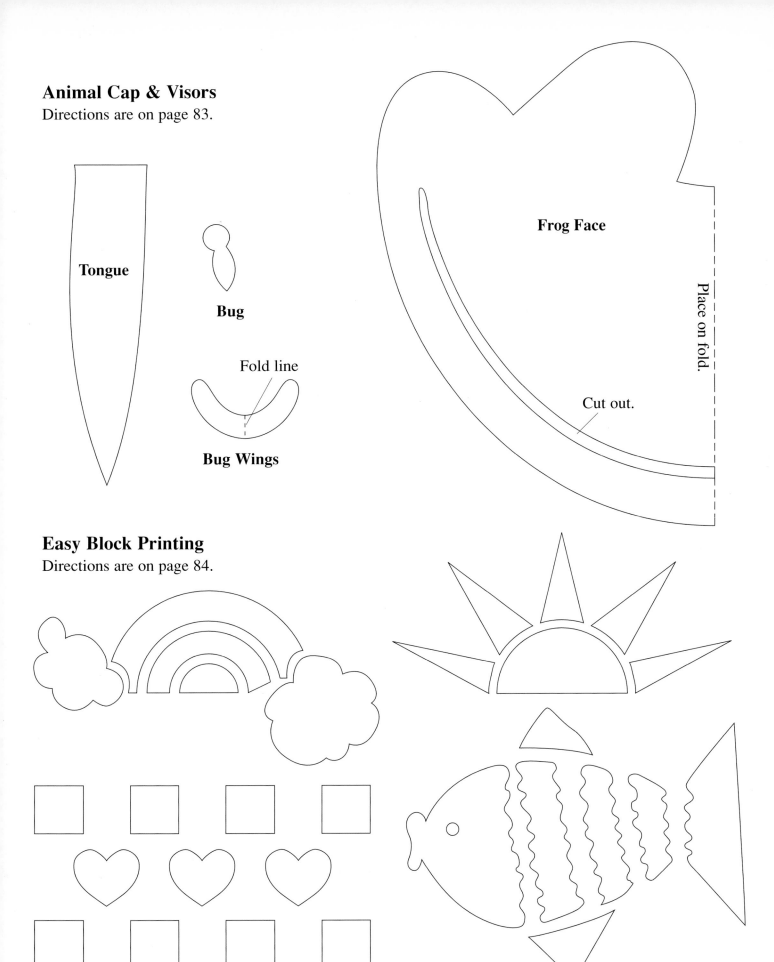

Tongue

Bug

Fold line

Bug Wings

Frog Face

Place on fold.

Cut out.

Easy Block Printing

Directions are on page 84.

Holiday Magic

Craft your way through the year with holiday decorations and wearables. Present your gifts in unique fused fabric boxes or easy decorated gift bags.

Christmas Tree Shirts

Prepare for the holidays by crafting a festive new shirt. Use the same fabrics to make matching outfits for mother and daughter.

Materials (for both)

For each: Patterns on page 126
Aleene's Fusible Web™
Cardboard covered with waxed paper
Gold glitter dimensional paint
For heart tree shirt: Adult-sized red sweatshirt
25 (2") squares assorted green Christmas print fabrics
For ornament tree shirt: Child-sized white T-shirt
Fabrics: assorted red print scraps, 3" square shiny gold
⅛"-wide red satin ribbon: 14 (6") lengths, 2 (26") lengths
Aleene's OK to Wash-It™ Glue
Large-eyed needle

Directions

Note: See page 136 for tips on working with fusible web.

1 **For each,** wash and dry shirt and fabrics; do not use fabric softener in washer or dryer.

2 **For heart tree shirt,** iron fusible web to wrong side of each Christmas print square. Transfer pattern to paper side of web on each square and cut 25 hearts. Referring to photo, fuse hearts to shirt front to form a tree shape. Place cardboard covered with waxed paper inside shirt. Embellish hearts with dimensional paint. Let dry.

3 **For ornament tree shirt,** iron fusible web to wrong side of red print and gold fabrics. Leaving a small tab at top of each circle for ornament hanger, cut the following from red fabric: 3 (1"-diameter) circles, 1 (1⅛"-diameter) circle, 2 (1¼"-diameter) circles, 3 (1½"-diameter) circles, 2 (1⅝"-diameter) circles, 1 (1¾"-diameter) circle, 1 (1⅞"-diameter) circle, 2 (2"-diameter) circles, and 3 (2¼"-diameter) circles. Transfer star pattern to paper side of web on gold fabric and cut out. Referring to *Ornament Tree Diagram,* fuse

ornaments to shirt front to form tree shape. Fuse star to shirt at top of tree. Place cardboard covered with waxed paper inside shirt. Embellish appliqués with dimensional paint (see photo). Let dry. Tie each 6" length of ribbon in a bow. Referring to photo, glue bows to shirt front. Let dry.

4 Thread needle with 1 (26") length of ribbon. Beginning approximately 1" from cuff at center top of 1 sleeve, make ¾"-long stitches around cuff. Gathering sleeve slightly, tie ribbon in a bow and knot ribbon ends. Repeat for other sleeve.

5 Do not wash shirt for at least 1 week. Turn shirt wrong side out, wash by hand, and hang to dry.

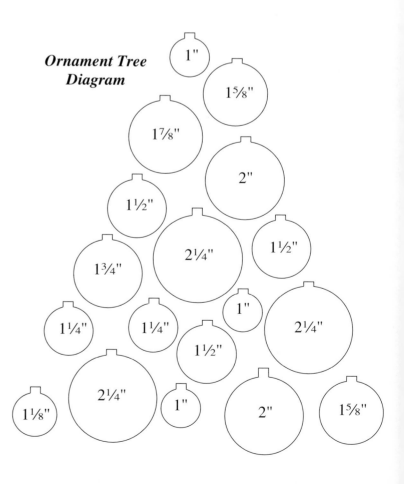

Ornament Tree Diagram

Quick Christmas Cards

Use the shapes from the Christmas Tree Shirts on page 100 to make these greeting cards.

Materials (for both)
For each: Aleene's Fusible Web™
For hearts card: Pattern on page 126
Green print fabric scraps
6⅛" x 7" piece beige paper
For ornaments card: Red print fabric scraps
5½" x 8¼" piece green paper
Dimensional paints: gold, green

Directions
Note: See page 136 for tips on working with fusible web.

1 **For each,** wash and dry fabric scraps, do not use fabric softener in washer or dryer. **For hearts card,** iron fusible web to wrong side of green print scraps. Transfer heart pattern to paper side of web and cut 3. Fold paper in half widthwise to form 3½" x 6⅛" card. Fuse hearts to card front.

2 **For ornaments card,** iron fusible web to wrong side of red print scraps. Leaving a small tab at top of each circle for ornament hanger, cut 1 (2¼"-diameter) circle, 1 (1½"-diameter) circle, and 1 (1"-diameter) circle. Fold paper in half widthwise to form 4⅛" x 5½" card. Referring to photo, fuse fabric ornaments to card front. Embellish card front with dimensional paints. Let dry.

Star Cards

These sponge-painted cards are a great bazaar item. Package 5 or 10 of them in a clear plastic bag and watch how fast they sell.

Materials (for 1 card)
Patterns on page 126
5½" x 8" piece paper
Aleene's Shrink-It™ Plastic
Waxed paper
Acrylic paint
Small sponge piece

Directions

1 Fold paper in half widthwise to form 4" x 5½" card. **For yellow stars card,** draw a 4" x 5½" rectangle on Shrink-It. Transfer patterns for stars A, B, and C to Shrink-It, positioning stars randomly within marked rectangle. Cut out stars and set aside for another use. Dip sponge into water and wring out excess water. Pour a puddle of paint on waxed paper. Dip sponge into paint and blot excess paint on paper towel. Align stencil on card front and use sponge to stencil stars with paint. Let dry.

2 **For green-and-white card,** transfer pattern for star D to Shrink-It and cut out. Dip sponge into water and wring out excess water. Pour a puddle of paint on waxed paper. Dip sponge into paint and blot excess paint on paper towel. Position Shrink-It star on card front as desired and sponge-paint around edges of star. Carefully reposition star and repeat until desired effect is achieved. Let dry.

Christmas Flag

Deck your halls with a fused fabric banner. Cheery Christmas prints on a bright red background declare happy holidays for everyone.

Materials
Alphabet on page 91
26" x 46" piece red fabric
Assorted green Christmas prints: 12" x 26" piece,
    12" x 22" piece, 12" x 18" piece, scraps
3 assorted brown print scraps
Aleene's Fusible Web™
Gold glitter dimensional paint
Gold glitter
26" length ⅜"-diameter wooden dowel
2 (1"-tall) wooden candle cups
Green acrylic paint
Paintbrush
Aleene's Professional Wood Glue™

Directions
Note: See page 136 for tips on working with fusible web.

1 Wash and dry fabrics; do not use fabric softener in washer or dryer. Fuse 1"-wide strips of fusible web to each edge on wrong side of red fabric. To hem flag, turn under 1" along both long sides and 1 short end and fuse. To make dowel casing, turn under 4" along remaining short end of fabric and fuse.

2 Iron fusible web to wrong side of remaining fabrics. To cut large tree from 12" x 26" green print fabric, draw a triangle 25" tall and 11" wide at base on paper side of web. Cut out. In same manner, draw a triangle 20½" tall and 11" wide at base on 12" x 22" green print fabric for medium tree and draw a triangle 17" tall and 11" wide at base on 12" x 18" green print fabric for small tree. Reverse letters for "happy holidays" so that they will be right side up when applied to flag. Transfer letters to paper side of web on green print scraps. Cut out. For each tree, cut 1 (2½" x 3½")

brown print piece for trunk. Referring to photo and *Flag Diagram,* fuse trees, tree trunks, and letters to flag. Embellish trees with gold glitter paint. Sprinkle wet paint with gold glitter. Let dry.

3 Paint dowel and candle cups green. Let dry. Slip dowel through casing in flag. Glue 1 candle cup to each end of dowel. Let dry.

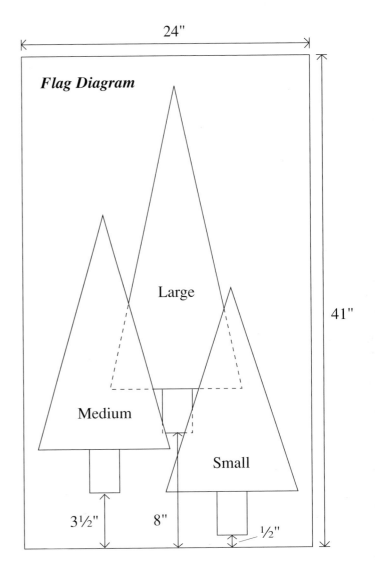

Flag Diagram

Large

Medium

Small

24"

41"

3½"

8"

½"

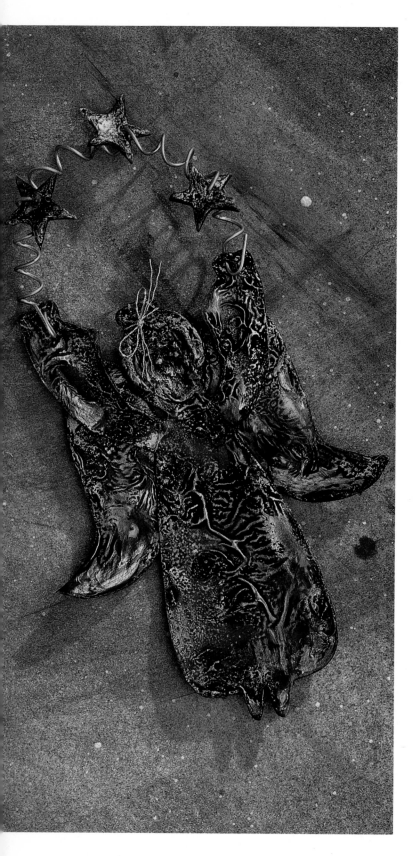

Burnt Brown Bag Angel

Highlights of gold paint enhance the texture of this beautiful ornament.

Materials
Patterns on page 127
Brown grocery bags
3" square cardboard for squeegee
Aleene's Tacky Glue™
Gold paste paint
Gold spray paint
15" length 18-gauge florist's wire
Ice pick
6" length gold metallic thread

Directions

1 Cut 2 (7") squares of brown bag. Using cardboard squeegee, apply 1 coat of glue to 1 side of 1 brown bag piece. With edges aligned, press remaining brown bag piece into glue. Transfer patterns to layered bag and cut 1 angel, 1 hair, 2 wings, and 3 stars.

2 Spread a fairly thick coat of glue on right side of each piece using fingers. Refer to Burnt Brown Bag How-to on pages 138 and 139 to burn each piece. Let dry. Dot glue on face for eyes. Let dry. To add gold highlights, rub finger in gold paste paint, wipe off excess on paper towel, and gently rub finger over each burned piece. Continue adding gold to each piece until desired effect is achieved. Let dry. Spray-paint florist's wire gold. Let dry.

3 Using ice pick and referring to patterns, poke 1 hole in each hand and star. Glue hair and wings in place on angel. Leaving 1" free at each end, twist wire around a pencil to coil. Remove pencil. Referring to photo, thread stars on wire and glue in place. Let dry. Thread 1 end of wire from back to front through each hole in hand. Bend each end of wire about ¾" at front of angel. Tie gold thread in a bow around hair.

Craft Stick & Buttons Ornament

This tiny stick tree decked with colorful buttons makes a perfect last-minute Christmas gift for anyone on your list.

Materials

5 wooden craft sticks
Aleene's Designer Tacky Glue™
Green acrylic paint
Paintbrush
7" length gold metallic thread
Buttons: 1 white star, 13 assorted sizes and colors

Directions

1 To make tree branches, cut 1 craft stick 1" from each end. Discard middle portion. Cut second craft stick 1½" from each end. Discard middle portion. Cut third craft stick 1¾" from each end. Discard middle portion. Glue 1 whole craft stick horizontally across remaining whole craft stick, ⅞" from 1 end. With cut ends butted together, glue 1¾" stick pieces in place, about ½" above whole stick (see photo). In same manner, glue remaining stick pieces in place to form tree. Let dry.

2 Paint tree green. Let dry. Fold gold thread in half to form a loop. Glue star button to top of tree, sandwiching gold thread ends between. Let dry. Glue remaining buttons to tree as desired. Let dry.

Paper Sculpture Ornaments

Use metallic paper to make a set of shimmering ornaments for your Christmas tree.

Materials (for both)

For each: Patterns on page 127
Hole punches: ⅛"-diameter, ³⁄₁₆"-diameter
Aleene's Tacky Glue™
Toothpick
10" length gold metallic thread
For gold ornament: 5½" square heavyweight
  gold metallic paper
Lightweight metallic paper scraps: red, green
For silver ornament: 5½" square heavyweight
  silver metallic paper
Lightweight paper scraps: glossy white, gold
  metallic

Directions

1 **For each,** transfer ornament pattern to heavyweight paper and cut out.

2 **For gold ornament,** transfer diamond pattern to red paper and cut 14. Punch 13 (³⁄₁₆"-diameter) circles from green paper. Referring to photo, center and punch 1 (³⁄₁₆") hole in each scallop of ornament; punch 2 (⅛") holes on each side of ³⁄₁₆" hole on each scallop of ornament. With right sides facing, fold each red diamond in half lengthwise and crease. Unfold diamonds. Cut 2 diamonds in half widthwise. Referring to photo, glue whole diamonds, half diamonds, and circles to ornament, using toothpick to apply glue. Let dry.

3 **For silver ornament,** transfer diamond pattern to white paper and cut 12. Punch 1 (³⁄₁₆"-diameter) circle from white paper. Punch 36 (³⁄₁₆"-diameter) circles from gold paper. Referring to photo, center and punch 1 (³⁄₁₆") hole in each

scallop of ornament; punch 1 (⅛") hole at bottom point of each scallop of ornament. With right sides facing, fold each diamond in half lengthwise and crease. Unfold diamonds. Referring to photo, glue diamonds, white circle, and gold circles to ornament, using toothpick to apply glue. Let dry.

4 **For each,** fold gold thread in half to form a loop and knot ends. Thread folded end of loop through 1 hole in ornament from back to front. Thread knotted ends through fold and pull tight to secure.

108

Fun Foam Huggers

Make these adorable huggers as favors for your next summertime celebration. They're perfect for holding cans on picnics or to decorate cups and glasses at the table.

Materials (for both)

For each: Patterns on page 128
¼"-diameter hole punch
Aleene's Designer Tacky Glue™
Clothespins
For panda: Fun Foam: 5½" x 9¾" rectangle black, 6½" square white, pink scrap, aqua scrap
For moon: Fun Foam: 3½" square yellow, white scrap, pink scrap, blue scrap, 4⅜" x 9¾" rectangle blue

Directions

1 **For panda,** center ears pattern 4⅜" from long bottom edge of black foam rectangle. Transfer ears pattern to foam, extending line at bottom edge of ears to each end of rectangle. Cut foam along pattern line. Transfer patterns and cut 1 face and 2 arms from white foam and 1 nose from pink foam. Punch 2 circles for eyes from aqua foam. Referring to photo, glue foam pieces in place on black foam. Let dry.

2 Curve foam into a cylinder, overlapping short ends ⅜", and glue. Use clothespins to hold ends together until glue is dry.

3 **For moon,** transfer patterns and cut 1 moon and 3 stars from yellow foam and 1 eye from white foam. Cut 1 (¾"-diameter) circle from pink foam. Punch 1 circle from blue foam scrap. Cut blue circle in half and discard 1 half. Referring to photo, glue foam pieces in place on blue foam rectangle. Let dry. Repeat Step 2 to complete hugger.

Seasonal Welcome Sign

Glue layers of brown bag together to craft a decoration for your door or foyer. Use the designs shown here to reflect the changing seasons or adapt other patterns to create ornaments for various holidays.

Materials (for all items shown)

For each: Patterns on pages 128 and 129
Brown grocery bags
3" square cardboard for squeegee
Aleene's Tacky Glue™
3/16"-diameter hole punch
Paintbrush

For banner: Alphabet on page 91
Acrylic paints: slate blue, ivory
Dimensional paints: slate blue, silver
30" length 18-gauge florist's wire

For flower basket: Acrylic paints: brown, lavender, pink, dark pink, green
Dimensional paints: light brown, lavender, light pink, pink, yellow, dark green

For heart: Acrylic paints: red, blue, white
Dimensional paints: red, silver

For autumn leaf: Acrylic paints: tan, dark brown, light brown, orange
Small sponge pieces
Copper dimensional paint

For snowman: Acrylic paints: black, white
Dimensional paints: black, green, orange
6" length red yarn

Directions

1 **For each,** glue 4 layers of brown grocery bag together, applying 1 coat of glue between layers using cardboard squeegee. Transfer patterns to layered bag and cut 1 banner, 1 W, 2 Es, 1 L, 1 C, 1 O, 1 M, 1 basket, 3 flowers, 9 leaves, 1 heart, 3 stars, 1 autumn leaf, and 1 snowman. Bend pieces to shape as desired. From remaining layered bag, cut 1 (1/8" x 3½") strip, 3 (3/8" x 2") strips, and 1 (½" x 1⅛") strip. Round 1 end of ½" x 1⅛" strip.

Let dry. Punch holes as indicated on patterns. Punch hole in rounded end of ½" x 1⅛" strip.

2 Paint autumn leaf with a base coat of tan acrylic paint. Let dry. Sponge-paint autumn leaf with dark brown, light brown, and orange, letting dry between colors. (See page 139 for tips on sponge painting.) Referring to photo for colors and using paintbrush, paint each remaining piece with acrylic paints. Let dry. Embellish pieces with dimensional paints as desired. Let dry.

3 **For banner,** glue letters to banner. Let dry. From wire, cut 1 (19") length and 1 (11") length. To make banner hanger, leaving 1" free at each end, twist 19" wire around a pencil to coil. Remove pencil. Thread 1 end of wire from front to back through each hole in top edge of banner. Bend each end of wire about ¾" at back of design. To make decoration hanger, leaving 1½" free at each end, twist 11" wire around a pencil to coil. Remove pencil. Bend each end of wire about ½" at each end. Hook 1 end of decoration hanger through hole in bottom edge of banner. Hang ornament on free wire hook.

4 **For flower basket,** glue leaves to flowers and flowers to basket (see photo). Let dry.

5 **For heart,** glue 1/8" x 3½" strip horizontally across center. Glue 3/8" x 2" strips vertically to bottom half of heart. Trim strips even with heart. Glue stars to heart. With hole positioned above edge of heart, glue ½" x 1⅛" strip to top back of heart. Let dry.

6 **For snowman,** knot yarn around neck for scarf and fray ends.

All Occasion Cards

Add a truly personal touch to your correspondence with handmade cards. Select fabric and paper in colors to suit your style or for a special occasion.

Materials (for 3 cards)

For fabric heart card: Pattern on page 126
Pink fabric scrap
5½" x 8" piece paper
Small wavy-edged scissors
Aleene's Fusible Web™
3" heart paper doily
10" length ½"-wide pink sheer ribbon
Aleene's Tacky Glue™

For fabric initial card: Alphabet on page 91
Pink fabric scrap
5½" x 8" piece paper
Wavy-edged scissors
Aleene's Fusible Web™
2½"-diameter paper doily

For punched hearts card: Pattern on page 130
Tracing paper
4¼" x 5½" piece heavyweight artist's paper
Scalloped-edge scissors
6" x 7" piece foam-core board or Styrofoam
Pearl-headed florist's pin
4½" x 5¾" piece paper with rounded corners
⅛"-diameter hole punch
10" length ⅛"-wide pink satin ribbon

Directions

Note: See page 136 for tips on working with fusible web.

1 **For fabric heart card and fabric initial card,** wash and dry fabrics; do not use fabric softener in washer or dryer. **For fabric heart card,** fold paper in half widthwise to form 4" x 5½" card. Using small wavy-edged scissors, trim ¼" from bottom edge of card front. Iron fusible web to wrong side of pink fabric scrap and heart doily. Transfer heart pattern to paper side of web on pink scrap and cut out. Center and fuse heart doily on card front. Center and fuse fabric heart on heart doily. Tie ribbon in a bow. Glue bow to card front.

2 **For fabric initial card,** fold paper in half widthwise to form 4" x 5½" card. Using wavy-edged scissors, trim ¼" from bottom edge of card front and back. Iron fusible web to wrong side of pink fabric scrap and doily. Reverse pattern for desired letter so that it will be right side up when applied to card. Transfer letter to paper side of web on pink scrap and cut out. Center and fuse doily on card front. Center and fuse fabric letter on doily.

3 **For punched hearts card,** transfer punched hearts design to tracing paper. Cut edges of 4¼" x 5½" paper piece with scalloped-edge scissors. Center and tape this paper piece on foam-core board or Styrofoam. Arrange tracing paper pattern on top of paper in desired position and tape to secure. Using florist's pin, punch design into paper. Remove tracing paper pattern. Remove punched paper piece from foam-core or Styrofoam. With right side up, lay punched paper piece on top of 4½" x 5¾" paper piece. Punch through both pieces to make 2 holes side by side in center of top edge. Thread ribbon through holes and tie in a bow on card front.

Fused Fabric Gift Boxes

To recycle a cardboard box, fuse on a bright print and embellish it with ribbons. Or select a theme print and coordinate the trimmings.

Materials (for 3 boxes)

For each: Print fabric
Aleene's Fusible Web™
Cardboard box
Aleene's Designer Tacky Glue™

For gardener's box: Raffia, miniature straw hat trimmed with ribbon and silk flowers, miniature gardening tools

For button box: Assorted ribbons, plastic beads, and plastic buttons to match fabric

For butterfly box: Ribbon to match fabric

Directions

Note: See page 136 for tips on working with fusible web.

1 **For each,** wash and dry fabric; do not use fabric softener in washer or dryer. Carefully open box until it lies completely flat. Iron fusible web to wrong side of fabric. Place flattened box right side down on paper side of web and trace. Cut out shape just outside marked lines. Center and fuse fabric on right side of box. Refold box into its original shape and glue flaps in place, leaving 1 end unglued.

2 **For gardener's box,** tie raffia in a bow around box. Glue hat and gardening tools to box. Let dry.

3 **For button box,** holding all lengths as 1, tie ribbons in a bow around box. String beads on ribbon ends and knot ends to secure. Glue buttons to box as desired. Let dry.

4 **For butterfly box,** tie ribbon in a bow around box. Cut butterfly motifs from fused fabric scraps and glue to ribbon and box. Let dry.

Pretty Gift Bags

Embellish gift bags with napkin appliqué motifs, fused fabric motifs, or paint to create a wrap for any occasion. A decorated bag, like the teacup one shown here, is the perfect way to present a theme gift.

Materials (for all 3)

For tea gift bag: Paper napkins with teacup motif
Aleene's Paper Napkin Appliqué™ Glue
Paintbrush
White gift bag
Dimensional paints: pink, light green, yellow, silver

For baby gift bag: Alphabet on page 91
Fabrics: baby motif cutouts, blue gingham scraps
Aleene's Fusible Web™
Pink gift bag
Dimensional paints: yellow, light green

For flower basket gift bag: Acrylic paints: brown, yellow, pink, purple, orange, green
Waxed paper
Basket-shaped plastic cookie cutter
Blue gift bag
4 pencils with erasers
Fine-tip paintbrush
Dimensional paints: orange, gold, blue, purple

Directions

1 For tea gift bag, cut teacup motifs from napkins. Remove bottom plies of napkins to leave cutouts 1 ply thick. Brush an even coat of glue on bag in desired position. Place cutout on glue-covered area and press out air bubbles. Gently brush top of cutout with a coat of glue. Repeat to apply additional napkin cutouts to bag. Let dry. Referring to photo, embellish bag with dimensional paints. Let dry.

2 For baby gift bag, wash and dry fabrics; do not use fabric softener in washer or dryer. Iron web to wrong side of baby motif cutouts and blue gingham. (*Note:* See page 136 for tips on working with fusible web.) Reverse letters for "baby" so that they will be right side up when applied to bag. Transfer letters to paper side of web on blue gingham and cut out. Fuse baby motif cutouts and letters to bag. Referring to photo, embellish bag with dimensional paints. Let dry.

3 For flower basket gift bag, pour a puddle of brown paint on waxed paper. Dip cookie cutter into paint and press on bag in desired position. Repeat to paint bag with additional baskets as desired. Let dry. To paint flowers on bag, pour a puddle of paint on waxed paper. Dip pencil eraser into paint and dot on bag. Use clean eraser for each color of paint. Repeat until desired effect is achieved. Let dry. Use fine-tip brush to paint leaves. Let dry. Use dimensional paints to paint bows on basket handles. Let dry.

Heidi's Hint

When you are working with dimensional paints, always be sure to shake the paint thoroughly to mix it and get it into the writing tip of the bottle. Test the flow on a scrap of paper before applying paint to your project. Squeeze the bottle firmly with consistent pressure to keep the paint flowing smoothly. To prevent splatters of paint, keep the writing tip pointed down to keep air bubbles from getting into the paint. It's a good idea to store your bottles with the cap end down so that they are always ready to use.

Easter Basket Picture

Cut egg shapes from Fun Foam to make a decorative picture for your home. Let your children decorate the eggs with paint, napkin appliqué motifs, or trims cut from foam scraps.

Materials

Pattern on page 130
10½" x 13½" wooden frame
3" square cardboard for squeegee
Aleene's Tacky Glue™
11½" x 14½" piece pink gingham
Fun Foam: white, pink, yellow, light green, brown
Dimensional paints: purple, turquoise, red, yellow, pink
Paper napkin cutouts: rabbit motif, pink flower motif, purple flower motif
Aleene's Paper Napkin Appliqué™ Glue
Paintbrush
Pinking shears
¼"-diameter hole punch
1½ yards ⅝"-wide pastel plaid ribbon
5" length 26-gauge florist's wire

Directions

1 Squeegee 1 side of frame cardboard backing with Tacky Glue. With glue side down, center cardboard on wrong side of fabric. Fold and glue excess fabric to cardboard, being sure fabric is taut. Let dry.

2 Transfer egg pattern to Fun Foam and cut 3 white, 2 pink, 2 yellow, and 2 light green. Referring to photo, embellish 2 white eggs, 1 yellow egg, and 1 light green egg with dimensional paints. Let dry. To apply rabbit motif to remaining white egg, purple flower motif to remaining yellow egg, and pink flower motif to 1 pink egg, brush an even coat of Napkin Appliqué Glue on foam in desired position. Place cutout on glue-covered area and press out air bubbles. Gently brush top of cutout with a coat of Napkin Appliqué Glue. Let dry. Embellish napkin appliqué eggs with dimensional paint as desired. Let dry. From foam scraps, use pinking shears and scissors to cut strips to decorate remaining eggs (see photo). Punch circles from white foam scraps for pink egg. Glue foam decorations in place on eggs using Tacky Glue. Embellish white circles on pink egg with dots of dimensional paint. Let dry.

3 From brown foam, cut 16 (½" x 6") strips and 1 (½" x 16") strip. Lay 11 (6") strips side by side on work surface. Weave 5 remaining 6" strips through these 11 strips to make basket. Glue strips together at edges using Tacky Glue.

4 Referring to photo, glue basket and eggs in place on fabric-covered cardboard using Tacky Glue. Let dry. Glue 16" strip of brown foam in place for basket handle using Tacky Glue. Let dry. Make a multilooped bow with ribbon, using florist's wire to secure bow. Glue bow to fabric-covered cardboard at top of basket handle using Tacky Glue. Let dry. Place picture in frame.

Halloween Shirt & Treat Bag

Celebrate Halloween in a sweatshirt decorated with glittery stenciled letters and fused fabric motifs.

Materials (for both)

For each: Aleene's Fusible Web™
For sweatshirt: Patterns on pages 130 and 131
Black adult-sized sweatshirt
Fabrics: 5" x 6" piece orange minidot, green scrap, 6" x 9" piece white
Cardboard covered with waxed paper
3 (4½" x 7½") pieces freezer paper
Aleene's OK to Wash-It™ Glue
Paintbrush
Fine glitter: gold, orange
Dimensional paints: green, orange, silver, black
For treat bag: Alphabet on page 91
Pattern on page 131
Fabrics: orange minidot scraps, bat motif cutouts
Black gift bag
Fun Foam scrap
Aleene's Tacky Glue™
Pencil with eraser
Yellow acrylic paint
Waxed paper

Directions

Note: See page 136 for tips on working with fusible web.

1 **For sweatshirt,** wash and dry shirt and fabrics; do not use fabric softener in washer or dryer. Iron fusible web to wrong side of fabrics. Transfer patterns to paper side of web and cut 1 jack-o'-lantern, 1 stem, and 1 ghost. Referring to photo, fuse pieces to shirt. Place cardboard covered with waxed paper inside shirt.

2 Center and transfer B pattern to 1 freezer paper piece and O pattern to each of 2 freezer paper pieces. Carefully cut out shaded portion of each pattern. Do not discard cutout pieces. Reassemble all pieces for B and arrange, wax side down, on shirt in desired position. Press with iron for a few seconds to adhere pieces to shirt. Carefully peel shaded portion of design away from shirt and discard. Brush a thin coat of OK to Wash-It Glue on shirt inside stencil. Sprinkle wet glue with gold glitter. Let dry. Shake off excess glitter. Remove freezer paper stencil. Repeat to stencil first O with orange glitter and remaining O with gold glitter. Using dimensional paints, outline edges of fabric appliqués and draw facial features on ghost. Let dry. Do not wash shirt for at least 2 weeks. Turn shirt wrong side out, wash by hand, and hang to dry.

3 **For treat bag,** wash and dry fabrics; do not use fabric softener in washer or dryer. Iron fusible web to wrong side of fabrics. Reverse letters for "my treat bag" so that they will be right side up when applied to bag. Transfer letters to paper side of web on orange minidot scraps. Cut out. Fuse bats and letters to bag. Transfer star pattern to Fun Foam scrap and cut out. Glue star to pencil eraser using Tacky Glue. Let dry. Pour a puddle of yellow paint on waxed paper. Dip foam star into paint and press on bag. Repeat until desired effect is achieved. Let dry.

Host a Clown Party

Craft a clown toss game and matching party favors for your child's birthday party. A decorated T-shirt (shown on the next page) completes the set.

Materials (for all items shown)

For toss game: Patterns on pages 132 and 133
Aleene's Designer Tacky Glue™
1 (42-ounce) oatmeal container with plastic lid
Felt: peach, red, white, black
1½"-diameter pom-poms: 1 red, 1 orange
Red yarn
1 (8-ounce) plastic tub with lid
Striped fabric: 4" x 37" strip, 12" x 19" piece, 6 (3½"-diameter) circles
Thread and needle
Rickrack: 18" length green, 17" length blue
18" length ⅞"-wide purple satin ribbon
Pinking shears
Sand

For 1 party favor: Patterns on page 132
Aleene's Designer Tacky Glue™
Toilet tissue tube
Lightweight cardboard scrap
5½" x 6" piece striped fabric
Felt: peach, red, black, yellow, purple
Pinking shears
2 (12-mm) wiggle eyes
½"-diameter pom-poms: 1 red, 1 pink
Red yarn

For shirt: Patterns on page 133
Aleene's Paper Napkin Appliqué™ Glue
Child-sized white T-shirt
Cardboard covered with waxed paper
Paper napkins: clown motif, red, green, orange, pink, purple
Disappearing-ink pen
Paintbrush
Assorted colors dimensional paint

continued on page 125

Directions

1 **For toss game,** use Designer Tacky Glue to assemble game. Transfer large clown mouth pattern to oatmeal container, with bottom of mouth 2" from bottom of container. Cut out. Glue peach felt to container to cover sides. Cut opening in felt, leaving ½" of felt around mouth opening. Fold excess felt to inside of container, clipping curves as needed, and glue. Let dry. Transfer patterns to felt and cut 1 red lips, 2 white eyes, and 2 black pupils. Cut 6 (¼"-wide) pieces from black for eye details. Referring to photo, glue lips, eyes, pupils, eye details, and red pom-pom nose in place on felt-covered container. Let dry. Cut 5"-long pieces of yarn and glue to top of container for hair. Let dry.

2 Center and glue bottom of plastic tub on bottom of oatmeal container. Let dry. Turn under ¼" along 1 long edge of 4" x 37" fabric strip and glue. Let dry. Run a gathering thread along remaining long edge of strip. Gather strip to fit around bottom of oatmeal container and secure thread. Glue gathered edge of fabric around container, covering bottom edge of peach felt and overlapping ends. Glue green rickrack around top of striped fabric, covering gathering thread and overlapping ends. Let dry. Tie ribbon in a bow and glue to clown (see photo). Let dry.

3 For hat, transfer large clown hat to 12" x 19" fabric piece and cut out. Curve hat into a cone shape, overlapping straight edges ¼", and glue. Let dry. Turn under ¼" around bottom edge of hat and glue. Glue orange pom-pom to hat tip. Let dry. Place oatmeal container lid inside hat, just above hemmed edge and glue. Let dry. Glue blue rickrack around bottom edge of hat, overlapping ends. Let dry.

4 For each game piece, with wrong sides facing, hold 2 fabric circles together as 1 and cut around circles with pinking shears. Squeeze a line of glue around edge of 1 circle on wrong side, leaving a 1" area unglued. With wrong sides facing, press matching fabric circle into glue. Let dry. Fill circle with sand and glue 1" opening closed. Let dry.

5 **For each party favor,** use Designer Tacky Glue to assemble party favor. Using tube as a guide, cut a circle of cardboard to fit 1 end of tube and glue to bottom. Let dry. With 1 (5½") edge of fabric extending ¼" beyond bottom of tube, glue fabric around tube, overlapping ends. Turn top edge of fabric to inside of tube and glue. Turn bottom edge of fabric to bottom of tube and glue. Let dry. Transfer patterns to felt and cut 1 peach face, 2 peach ears, 1 red small clown mouth, 2 black crosses for eyes, 1 yellow tie, 1 yellow tie knot, and 1 purple small clown hat. Cut 1 (⅝" x 6¾") strip from remaining red felt, cutting 1 long edge of strip with pinking shears. Referring to photo, glue face, ears, mouth, crosses, wiggle eyes, red pom-pom nose, tie, and tie knot in place on fabric-covered tube. Let dry. Cut 1¼"-long pieces of yarn and glue to top of tube for hair. Let dry.

6 Curve hat into a cone shape, overlapping straight edges ¼", and glue. Let dry. With pinked edge at top, glue red strip around bottom of hat. Glue pink pom-pom to hat tip. Let dry.

7 **For shirt,** use Napkin Appliqué Glue to apply cutouts to shirt. Wash and dry shirt; do not use fabric softener in washer or dryer. Place cardboard covered with waxed paper inside shirt. Cut clown motifs from paper napkin. Transfer patterns to napkins and cut 1 large star each from red, green, orange, pink, and purple; 1 medium star from purple; 2 medium stars from green; 2 small stars from pink; and 1 small star each from red and orange. Remove bottom plies of napkins to leave cutouts 1 ply thick.

8 Referring to photo, place cutouts on shirt front. Using disappearing-ink pen, lightly trace around cutouts. Remove cutouts. Brush an even coat of glue on shirt front inside 1 traced line. Place cutout on glue-covered area and press out air bubbles. Lightly brush top of cutout with a coat of glue. Repeat to apply remaining napkin cutouts to shirt front. Let dry. Referring to photo, embellish napkin cutouts and shirt front with dimensional paints. Let dry. Do not wash shirt for at least 1 week. Turn shirt wrong side out, wash by hand, and hang to dry.

Christmas Tree Shirts
Directions are on page 100.

Quick Christmas Cards
Directions are on page 102.

All Occasion Cards
Directions are on page 112.

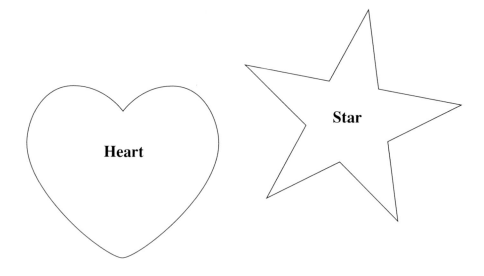

Star Cards
Directions are on page 103.

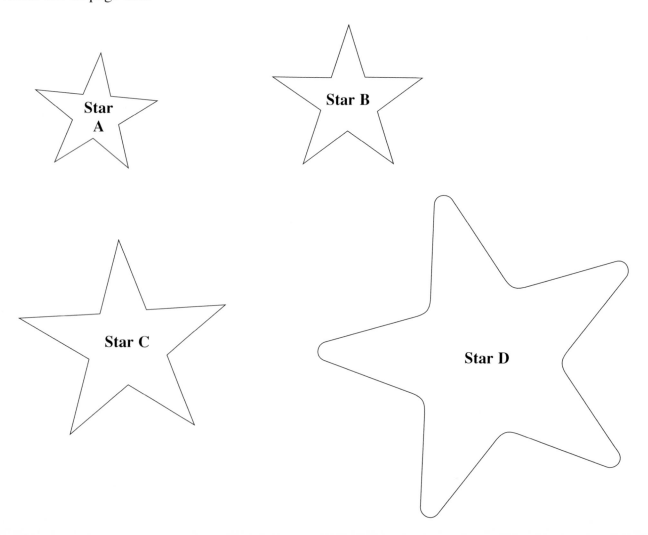

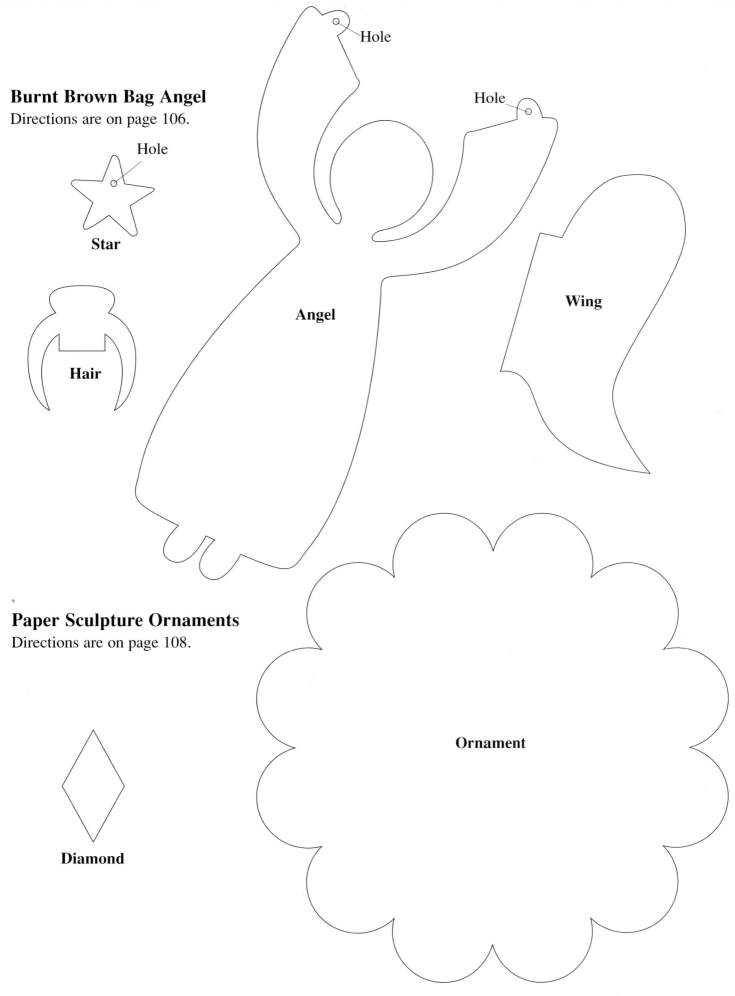

Burnt Brown Bag Angel

Directions are on page 106.

Hole

Star

Hair

Hole

Hole

Angel

Wing

Paper Sculpture Ornaments

Directions are on page 108.

Diamond

Ornament

Fun Foam Huggers
Directions are on page 109.

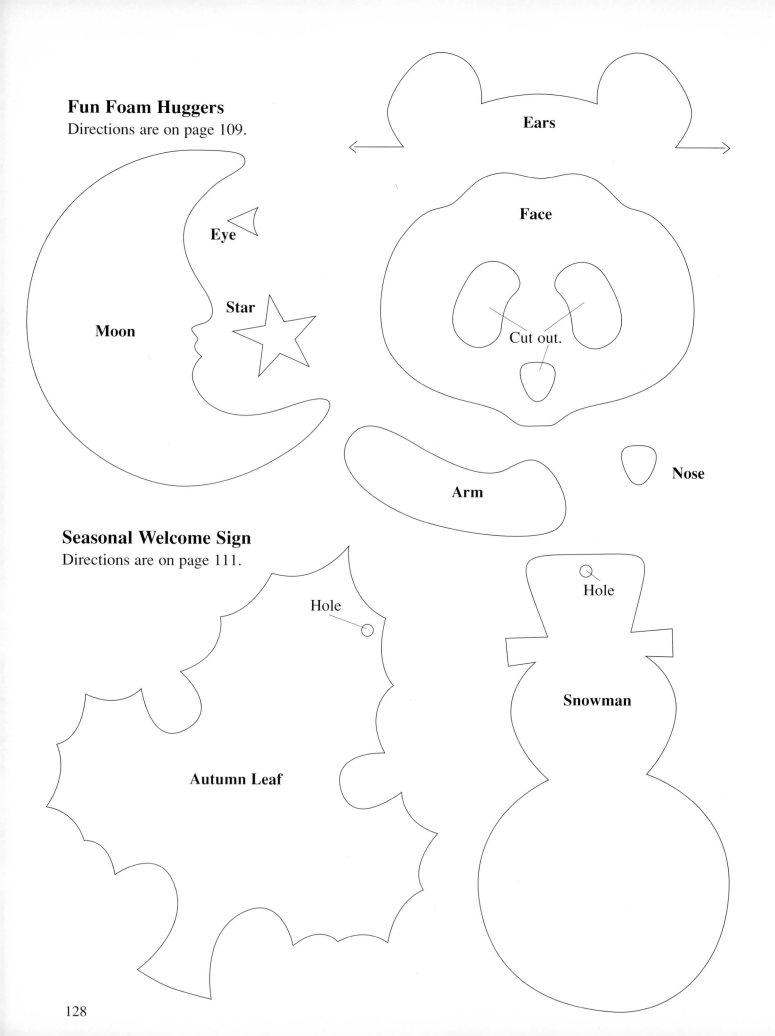

Ears

Eye

Face

Moon

Star

Cut out.

Nose

Arm

Seasonal Welcome Sign
Directions are on page 111.

Hole

Hole

Autumn Leaf

Snowman

Seasonal Welcome Sign
Directions are on page 111.

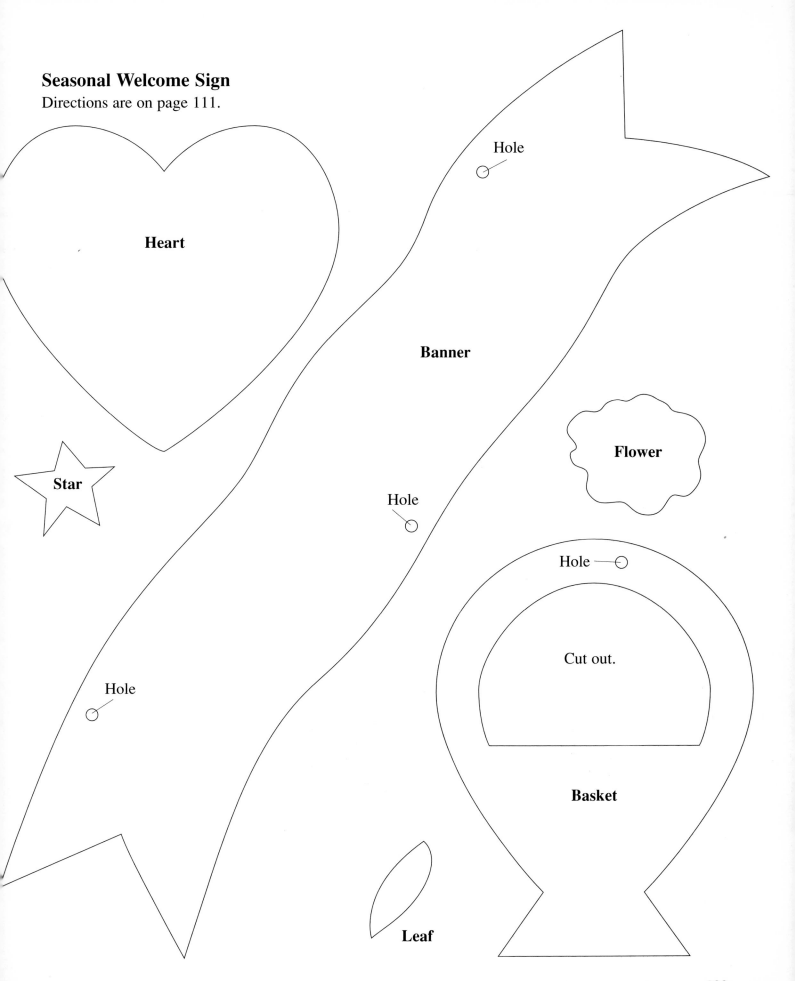

Heart

Hole

Banner

Star

Flower

Hole

Hole

Hole

Cut out.

Basket

Hole

Leaf

All Occasion Cards

Directions are on page 112.

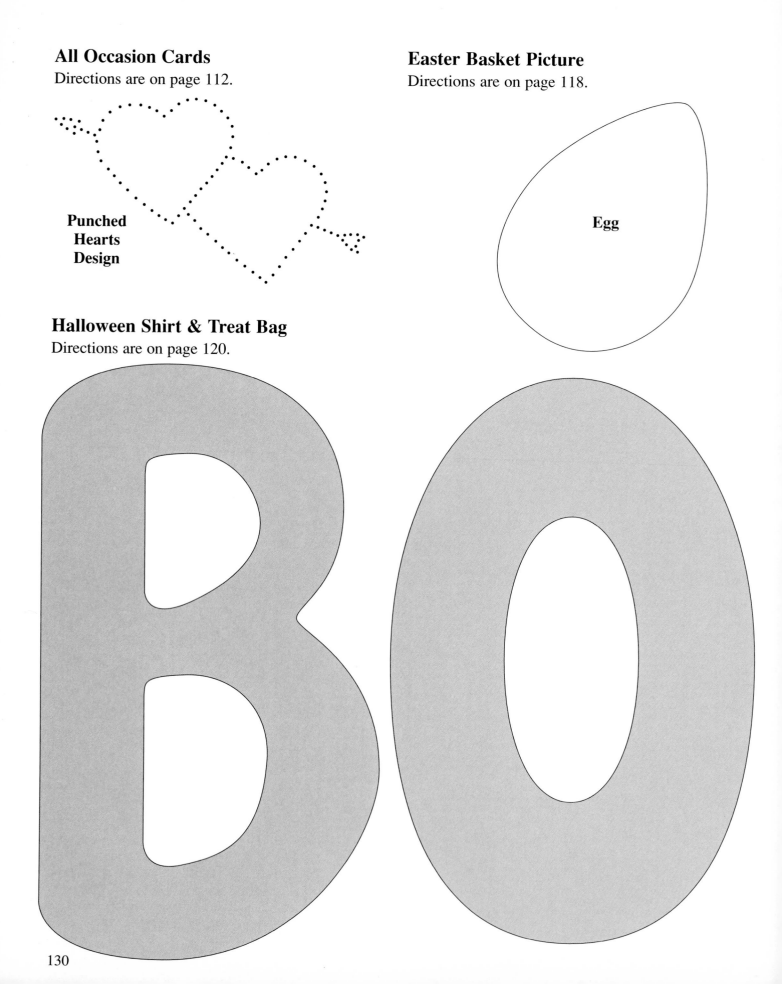

**Punched
Hearts
Design**

Easter Basket Picture

Directions are on page 118.

Egg

Halloween Shirt & Treat Bag

Directions are on page 120.

Halloween Shirt & Treat Bag
Directions are on page 120.

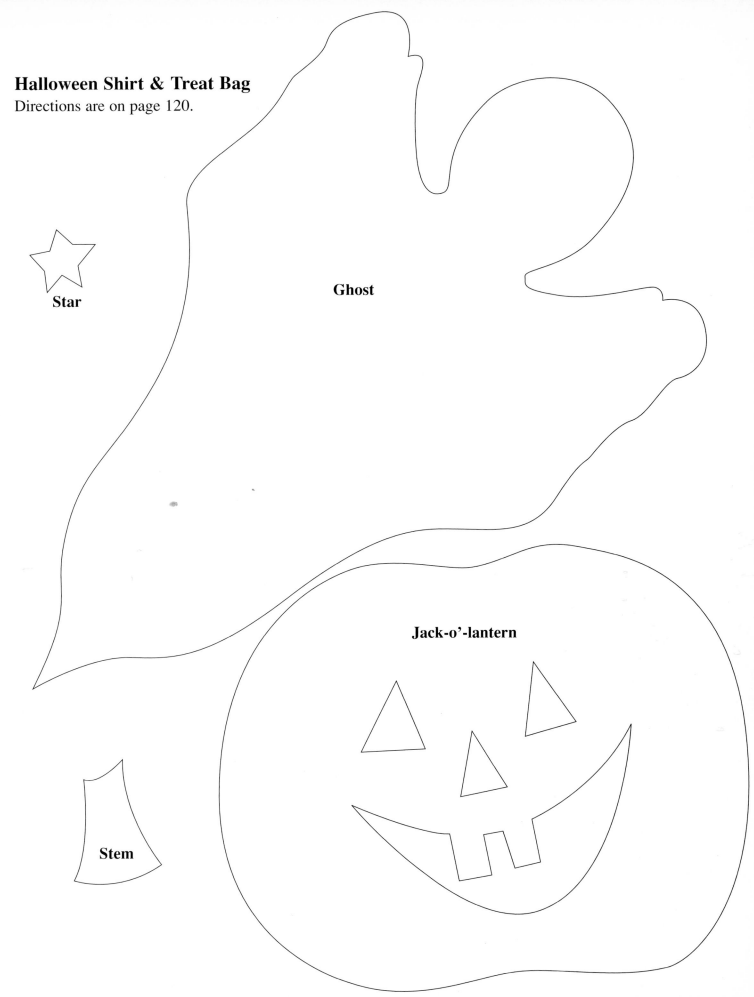

Star

Ghost

Jack-o'-lantern

Stem

Host a Clown Party
Directions are on pages 122–125.

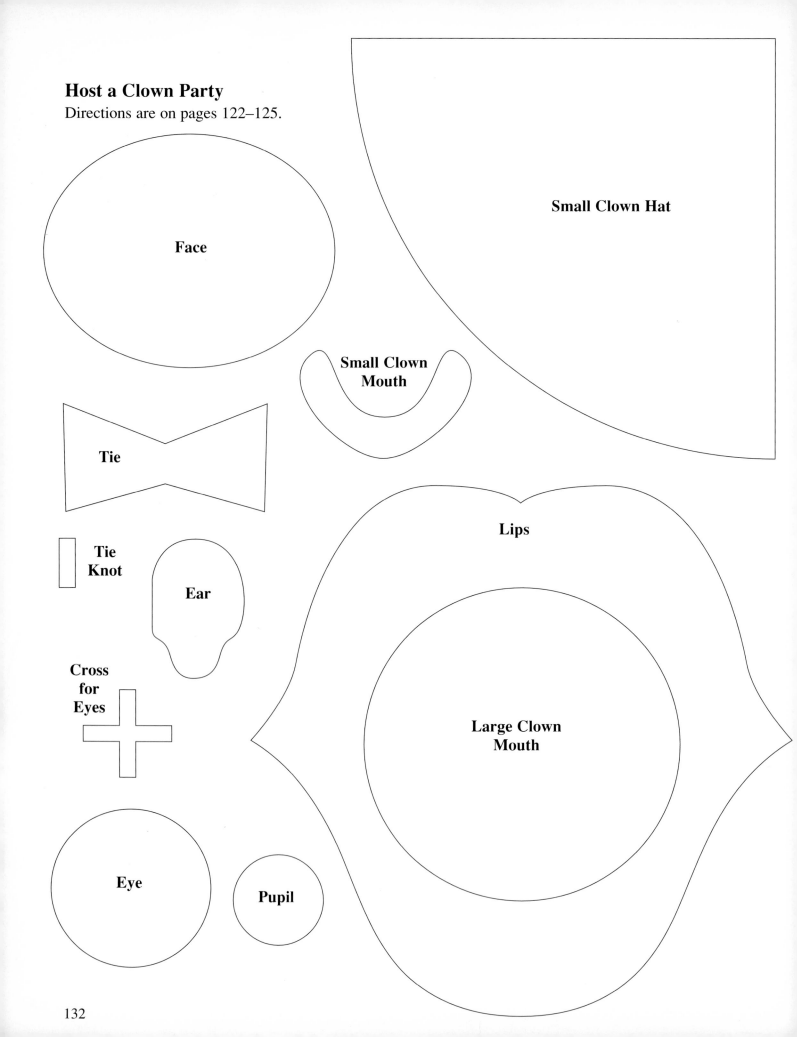

Face

Small Clown Hat

Small Clown Mouth

Tie

Lips

Tie Knot

Ear

Cross for Eyes

Large Clown Mouth

Eye

Pupil

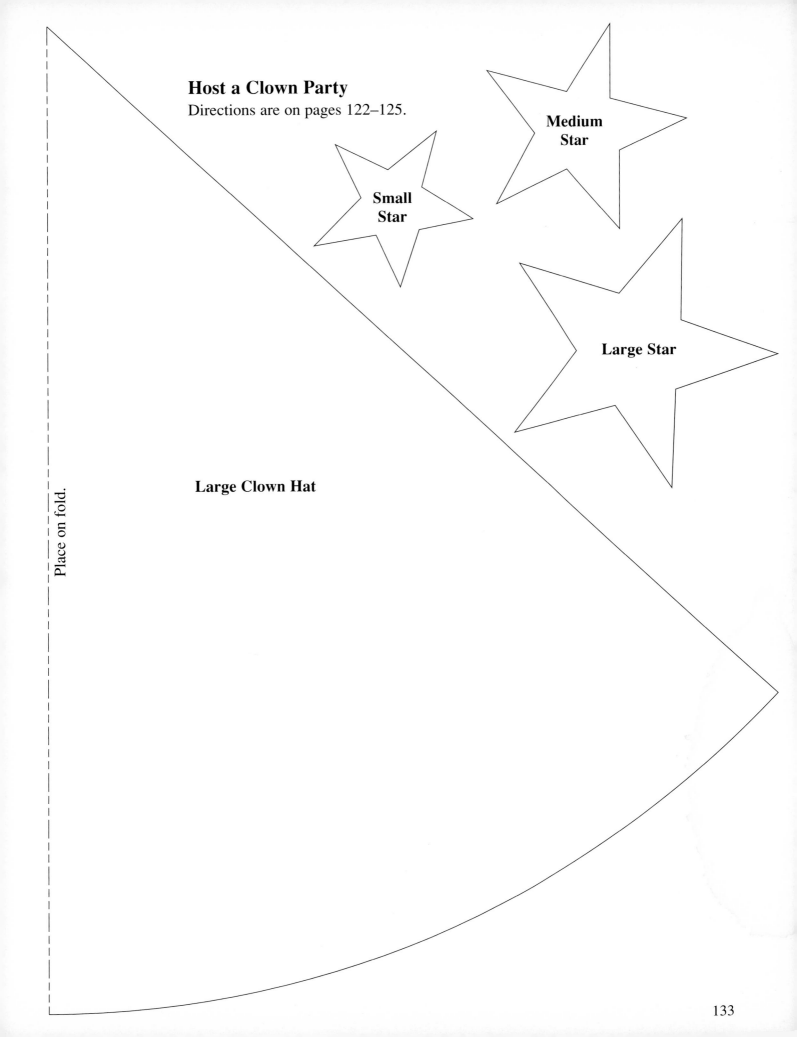

Host a Clown Party

Directions are on pages 122–125.

Medium Star

Small Star

Large Star

Large Clown Hat

Place on fold.

Crafting with Heidi

From making bread dough roses to burning brown bags, Heidi shares her wealth of crafting know-how in the following pages.

General Supplies

Here are some of the general supplies you'll need to have on hand for making many of the craft projects in this book.
- Waxed paper
- Florist's pins and straight pins
- Corrugated cardboard
- Several 3" squares of lightweight cardboard for squeegees
- Paper towels
- White paper, tracing paper, or Shrink-It Plastic for transferring patterns
- Ruler or measuring tape
- Pencils and colored pencils
- Paintbrushes (½" shader, fine-tip, and sponge brushes)
- Several pieces of pop-up craft sponge
- Fine-tip permanent black marker
- Rubber bands, clothespins, and large paper clips to hold things together while glue is drying
- Scissors (separate scissors for fabric, all-purpose scissors for use with paper and other craft materials, and heavy-duty scissors or wire cutters for use with florist's wire and other hard-to-cut items, as well as decorative blade scissors)
- Hole punches (⅛"-diameter, ³⁄₁₆"-diameter, ¼"-diameter, and decorative punches)
- Florist's wire (26-gauge for making bows and 18-gauge for use with other projects)
- Masking tape and transparent tape
- Fine-grade sandpaper
- Sewing needle and thread
- Toothpicks
- Disappearing-ink pen

- Purchased cardboard shirt form or cardboard covered with waxed paper for use with wearables
- Needlenose pliers

If you don't already have some of these items, don't feel you have to buy them all at once. It takes a while to accumulate a well-stocked crafting tool-box. Watch for sales or other discounts to buy your tools and supplies. Before you know it, you will have acquired all sorts of handy items for use in making crafts.

Choosing Your Glue

In each of the projects in this book, Heidi relied upon the extensive line of Aleene's products for her craft-making. To help you determine which glue is best suited for your general crafting, refer to the handy list below.

• Aleene's Tacky Glue™ is an excellent all-purpose glue for crafting. It is especially suited for working with fabric but not for use with wearables, because it is not washable.

• Aleene's Designer Tacky Glue™ is a thicker, tackier version of Tacky Glue and is intended for use with hard-to-hold items like Fun Foam.

• Aleene's Jewel-It™ and OK to Wash-It™ glues are designed for use with wearables and other fabric items that will need to be washed. In particular, use Jewel-It to adhere acrylic jewels or decorative buttons to wearables or home decor items.

The glues are nontoxic and ACMI (Art and Craft Materials Institute) approved, so they are safe for children to use. The glues dry clear and flexible, making them excellent for crafting.

Many of Aleene's products are available in crafts and hobby stores. All of the Aleene's products are available in Aleene's Crafts in the Mail Catalog. To receive a copy of the catalog, please send a $2.00 check or money order to Aleene's Catalog, Box 9500, Buellton, CA 93427.

Glue Hints & Tips

To make Tacky Glue or Designer Tacky Glue even tackier, leave the lid off for about an hour before you use the glue. This allows some of the moisture to evaporate. Do not dip a paintbrush or other item into the glue bottle as this will contaminate the glue and may cause mold to grow in the closed bottle. Instead pour a puddle of glue on a piece of waxed paper.

Do not use too much glue. Excess glue only makes the items slip around; it does not provide a better bond. To keep from applying too much glue when gluing together pieces of fabric or brown bag, use a cardboard squeegee to apply a film of glue to the surface. Simply cut a 3" square of cardboard (cereal box cardboard works well) and use the cardboard square to squeegee the glue onto the craft material. Wait a few minutes to let the glue begin to form a skin before putting the items together.

To apply consistent fine lines of glue to a project, use either the Aleene's Fine-Line Syringe Applicator, following the package directions, or see page 65 to make a tape tip for your glue bottle.

To use Jewel-It to attach a jewel or a button to a project, squeeze a puddle of glue on the project where you want your jewel to be placed. Press the jewel into the glue puddle, so that the glue comes up around the sides of the jewel.

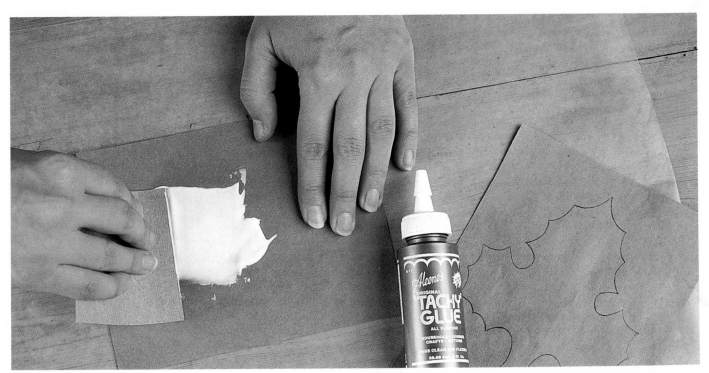

Working with Fusible Web

Aleene's Fusible Web™ makes no-sew projects faster and easier to accomplish. For the best results, always wash and dry fabrics and garments to remove any sizing before applying fusible web. Do not use fabric softener in the washer or the dryer.

Lay the fabric wrong side up on the ironing surface. A hard surface, such as a wooden cutting board, will ensure a firmer bond. Lay the fusible web paper side up on the fabric (the glue side feels rough). With a dry iron set on a hot setting, fuse the web to the fabric by placing and lifting the iron. Do not allow the iron to rest on the web for more than 1 or 2 seconds. Do not slide the iron back and forth across the web. Remember, you are only transferring the glue web to the fabric, not completely melting the glue.

Transfer the pattern to the paper side of the web and cut out the pattern as specified in the project directions. Or referring to the right side of the fabric, cut out the desired motif from a print fabric.

To fuse the appliqué to the project, carefully peel the paper backing from the appliqué, making sure the web is attached to the fabric. If the web is still attached to the paper, re-fuse it to the appliqué before fusing the appliqué to the project. Arrange the appliqué on the prewashed fabric or other surface as listed in the project directions. If you are fusing more that 1 appliqué, place all the appliqués in the desired position before fusing.

With a dry iron set on a hot setting, fuse the appliqués to the project by placing and lifting the iron. Hold the iron on each area of the appliqués for approximately 5 seconds. It is not necessary to apply paint to the edges of your fused appliqués, but using lines of dimensional paint provides a finished look to the appliqués.

Handmade Means Hand-Wash

After you have created a beautiful wearable, you will want to care for it properly. Be sure to let the glue or the paint on your new outfit dry for at least 1 week before washing. This allows the embellishment to form a strong bond with the fabric.

To wash, turn the garment wrong side out, hand wash, and hang to dry. Hand washing protects your hard work from the rough-and-tumble treatment of a washing machine.

Transferring Patterns

Before you begin any project, you should first read the directions all the way through. Also look at the patterns for additional important information. After you have familiarized yourself with the directions and the patterns, and have gathered all the necessary materials and supplies as listed in the materials list or the directions, you are ready to begin work on your chosen design.

Your first step in making a craft project usually involves transferring a pattern from the book to your craft material. To transfer a pattern, lay a piece of tracing paper or lightweight white paper (for a longer-lasting pattern, use Aleene's Opake Shrink-It™ Plastic instead) on top of the printed pattern. Trace the pattern using a pencil or a marker. Be sure to transfer any details, such as placement markings and facial features, to the tracing paper. Cut out the traced pattern.

When only half a pattern is given, fold the tracing paper in half and place the fold on the broken line of the pattern. Trace the pattern as printed and cut out through both layers. Unfold the paper for the complete pattern.

To transfer the pattern to the craft material, such as fabric, wood, or brown grocery bag, lay the pattern on the material as specified in the directions. Trace using a pencil or a pen for paper, wood, or cardboard and a disappearing-ink fabric marker for fabrics.

To reverse a pattern (like the alphabet on page 91), trace and cut out the pattern as described above. To transfer the pattern to the paper side of fusible web or to a print fabric, lay the pattern right side down on the paper side of the web or the wrong side of the fabric; then trace and cut out. To reverse a pattern to make a matched set of pieces (like the Burnt Brown Bag Angel's wings, see pages 106 and 127), trace the pattern piece onto the craft material once and then flip the pattern over and trace again. When your craft material has no right or wrong side, it is not necessary to reverse or to flip the pattern.

Heidi's Top Picks

Many of the projects in this book are perfect items for you to make for the next charity bazaar. (You might also want to make some things to sell for pin money.) Likewise a lot of these designs are appropriate for use with children. Whether you are a scout leader or a teacher, or if you just want to teach your children how to create homemade gifts, you'll find lots of choices in these pages.

Since many of these designs use ordinary household items, you'll also be showing youngsters a fun way to recycle. Here are Heidi's recommendations for crafts to make for a bazaar or to share your joy of crafting with children.

Great Bazaar Ideas
• *Sunny Setting* (pages 24 and 25): Sunflowers are very popular in home decorating. Offer place mats and napkin rings for sale in sets or as single items.
• *Window Screen Jewelry* (page 45): This lightweight jewelry accented with shimmering metallic paint will sell quickly.
• *Animal Cap & Visors* (pages 82 and 83): Decorated hats will be a hit with the kids.
• *Craft Stick & Buttons Ornament* (page 107): Inexpensive materials make this ornament a sure-fire money-maker.
• *Pretty Gift Bags* (pages 116 and 117): Display these decorated bags next to gift items to attract additional sales.

Perfect for Kids to Craft
• *Beaded Frames* (page 31): Glue beads and buttons to inexpensive frames for a super-quick gift idea.
• *Flowery Shoes & Cap* (page 49): These are so easy, even young children can make them.
• *Easy Block Printing* (pages 84 and 85): Encourage your children to design their own stamps.
• *Tic-tac-toe & Checkers Set* (pages 86 and 87): This colorful game set is Heidi's favorite project.
• *Fun Foam Huggers* (page 109): Commemorate a spend-the-night party with these huggers. Let the guests help craft them for a group activity.

Burnt Brown Bag How-to

Many years ago, during a flammability test of Tacky Glue, the product testers discovered that burning a layer of wet glue resulted in a surface resembling metal sculpture. With these step-by-step directions, you'll learn how to do this simple technique.

To do burnt brown bag projects (such as the wind chimes on page 26 or the angel on page 106), you will need to gather the supplies mentioned in the materials list for the specific project. You will also need: Aleene's Tacky Glue™, a candle, matches, and a scrap of fabric.

2 While the glue is still wet, hold the design, glue side down, directly over a candle flame. Hold the design as close to the flame as possible but don't snuff out the flame. Move the design around over the flame until all of the glue is black and sooty. (*Note:* The burning process takes 1½ to 2 minutes and will produce a little smoke.)

1 Glue together layers of brown grocery bag and cut out the pattern as specified in the project directions. Let dry. Spread a fairly thick coat of glue on 1 side of the brown bag shape.

3 Using a scrap of fabric, gently wipe away the soot. If any brown bag shows through, the glue is not completely burned; hold the design over the flame again to finish the burning process. To create a textured surface, use the fabric scrap to mold the soft glue, slightly ruffling the surface. Let the design dry overnight.

4 To add gold metallic highlights to a burnt brown bag design (see the wind chimes on page 26 or the angel on page 106), squeeze a puddle of gold paste paint on a piece of waxed paper. Dip your finger in the paint and wipe off the excess paint on a paper towel. Gently rub your finger over the burnt design. Continue adding gold to the design until the desired effect is achieved. Let the design dry. To sponge-paint a burnt brown bag design, refer to the sponge-painting tips below. Be sure to allow some of the black on the design to show through the paint to achieve a verdigris metal look (see the candle holders on page 21).

Sponge-Painting Tips

To sponge-paint a design, dip a small sponge piece into water to dampen it and wring out the excess water. Pour a puddle of 1 color of paint on a piece of waxed paper. Dip the sponge into the paint and blot the excess paint on a paper towel. Lightly press the sponge on the design. Repeat until the desired effect is achieved. Remember to apply the paint sparingly at first, because you can always add more paint to the design.

Sponge-paint small areas at a time and apply the paint in a random pattern. When using 3 or 4 colors of paint, begin with the darkest color. To achieve a layered look, leave some areas unpainted, allowing the background to show through. Always let each color of paint dry before applying the next or your work will become muddy and the colors will not be distinct. When applying additional colors of paint, overlap them a bit.

Do not allow your sponge to become saturated with paint. If the sponge becomes saturated, rinse it thoroughly in clean water and wring out the excess water.

Bread Dough How-to

Bread dough roses are featured in the Bread Dough Rose Frame on page 28 and in the Rose Button Covers & Pin on page 44. These delicate porcelain-like flowers are very easy to make, and all that you'll need to get started is a slice of white bread and a tablespoonful of Tacky Glue.

It is helpful to look at a real rose (or a picture of a rose) when making these flowers. But you can make your roses any color you wish so don't be limited by the colors you see in a garden. Light lavender or pale aqua might be the color you need to complement a blouse or to add a touch of color to your design.

1 To make 1 batch of basic bread dough, you will need 1 slice of white bread with the crust removed, 1 tablespoon of Aleene's Tacky Glue™, a plastic cup, a wooden craft stick, and acrylic paint as specified in the project directions. Break the bread into small pieces and put the pieces in a plastic cup. Add 1 tablespoon of glue to the bread and mix with the craft stick just until a coarse ball forms. (*Hint:* If you coat your tablespoon with cold cream, the glue will come off more easily.) Remove the ball of dough from the cup.

With clean hands, knead the dough for about 5 minutes or until it is smooth and pliable. (*Note:* Be sure to wash your hands because dirt on your hands will be transferred to the dough. If desired, rub your hands with cold cream to make the dough easier to work.) If the dough is too coarse, add a little more glue. The dough will stick to your hands until it becomes smooth.

2 To color the dough, divide the dough ball into a separate ball for each color of paint. Flatten 1 ball in your hand, making a small well in the center. Pour a small amount of acrylic paint in the well. Knead the dough in your hands until the paint is thoroughly incorporated. For deeper colors, add more paint to the dough, a little at a time, until the desired shade is achieved. Store each color of dough in a separate plastic bag. Bread dough can be stored overnight in the refrigerator.

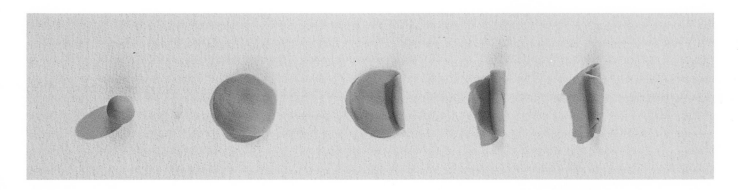

3 To make a rose, you will need a small ball of dough, colored according to the specific project directions. Pinch off a pea-sized piece of dough. Squeeze the pea between your forefinger and thumb to flatten it into a small, round piece the thickness of a piece of paper. (The thinner the petals, the more the finished rose will resemble porcelain.) To make the center of the rose, roll the flattened piece between your fingers, turning the top edge back slightly to look as if the rose were just beginning to unfurl.

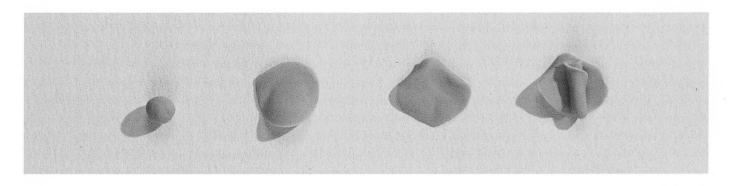

4 For the first petal, pinch off another pea-sized piece of dough and flatten it as before. Press the top edge back slightly to make a petal. Place the rose center in the center of this petal and wrap the petal around the center, gently pressing them together at the bottom.

5 Make another petal in the same manner. Place this petal opposite the first petal. If possible, look at a real rose while making your bread dough rose. Remember, not all rose petals are the same size.

6 Add 8 more petals, overlapping the edges slightly, to complete the rose. Place subsequent petals a bit higher on the rose, so that the turned back edges are even with the rose center.

Let the rose air-dry overnight. To glue the rose to a flat surface, cut off the bottom of the rose before it dries completely.

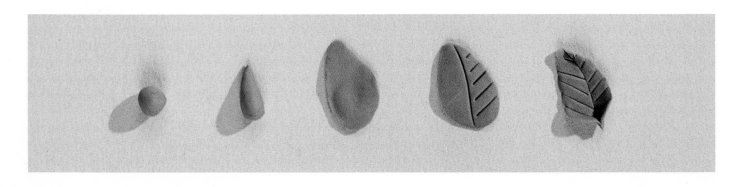

7 To make a leaf, you will need a small ball of green dough. Pinch off a pea-sized piece and mold it into a teardrop shape. Flatten the teardrop so that it is a bit thicker than a piece of paper. Using a straight pin or a scrap of Aleene's Shrink-It™ Plastic, make indentations in the top of the leaf for the veins. Holding the edge of the

pin or the plastic straight up, gently push into the edges of the leaf at the end of each vein to give the edges a jagged appearance. Curl and shape the leaf as desired and let it dry overnight. If desired, press the leaf in place at the bottom of the rose before they dry.

Shrink-It How-to

With Aleene's Shrink-It™ Plastic, you can make jewelry, refrigerator magnets, and many other kinds of crafts. Children will especially enjoy watching the designs shrink during baking. Be sure to keep the following tips in mind when working with Shrink-It.

Thoroughly sand the Shrink-It with fine-grade sandpaper before using colored pencils to color your design. Colored pencils will not adhere to Shrink-It that has not been sanded. Hold your sanded Shrink-It up to a light source to check for any unsanded areas.

Also remember to cut out your design and punch any holes as specified in the project directions before you shrink the design. After shrinking, your design will be very hard and you will not be able to cut it with scissors or to punch holes with a hole punch. If desired, wear a pair of cotton gloves to protect your hands while handling hot Shrink-It.

2 The edges of the design should begin to curl within 25 seconds. If the edges do not curl in 25 seconds, increase the temperature slightly. If the edges begin to curl as soon as the design is put in the oven, reduce the temperature. The design will curl and roll while it is shrinking. A large design may curl over onto itself. If this happens, open the oven and unfold the design; then continue baking.

1 Preheat a toaster oven or a conventional oven to 275° to 300°. Sprinkle a room-temperature baking board or nonstick cookie sheet with baby powder. (The baby powder prevents the design from sticking to the baking surface and ensures even shrinking.) Place the Shrink-It design on the prepared surface and put it in the oven.

3 After about 1 minute, the design will lie flat. Use a hot pad to remove the baking board from the oven. Use a spatula to move the design from the baking board to a flat surface. To keep the design flat during cooling, place a book on top of it. The design may be shaped before it cools. If you are not happy with the shape of your design after it has cooled, return it to the oven for a few seconds to warm it again. Remove the design from the oven and reshape it while it is still hot. Then set it aside to cool completely.

INDEX